T0305002

ARMAN AZADI

ACROSS MOUNTAINS, LAND & SEA

First published in Great Britain in 2024 by Trapeze,
an imprint of The Orion Publishing Group Ltd
Carmelite House, 50 Victoria Embankment
London EC4Y 0DZ

An Hachette UK Company

1 3 5 7 9 10 8 6 4 2

ISBN (Hardback) 978 1 4091 9932 8
ISBN (Export Trade Paperback) 978 1 4091 9933 5
ISBN (eBook) 978 1 4091 9935 9
ISBN (Audio) 978 1 4091 9936 6

Typeset by Born Group
Printed and bound in Great Britain by Clays Ltd, Elcograf S.p.A.

www.orionbooks.co.uk

This book is dedicated to my mother and those who cannot tell their stories.

Contents

Author's Note

I have changed details of some names, places and incidents to respect the privacy and maintain the safety of those I have known. Despite these changes, this book is an authentic representation of my experiences as I remember them. In 2022, the UNHCR (United Nations High Commissioner for Refugees) announced that for the first time since records had begun, a hundred million people were displaced by war, violence, persecution and human rights abuses.

PROLOGUE
Dover

When the lorry stopped, I climbed down from where I was hidden and stumbled out onto the concrete. My hands hurt from holding on. The cold morning breeze blew my greasy hair over my face.

'Hey!'

A few metres away, I saw a man in a glowing yellow jacket striding towards me. He was shouting something I didn't understand. I sat, too exhausted to run, as white birds cried above us. He stood over me.

'Do you speak English?'

I nodded.

'A little.'

Behind him, the sun rose, bright, and I squinted up at him. My mouth was dry. I wondered if he would beat me.

'Where are you from?'

He asked again, his voice gentler.

'Where are you from?'

Part One

1

Afghanistan

I was born in a house with bullet holes in the walls. Just before dawn, in the middle of a winter in the mountains of central Afghanistan. My mother, whose response to any news, however bad, was: 'God is kind', gave birth to me alone in the freezing darkness. I imagine first her, then my cries echoing through the empty valley, our animals lifting their heads with curiosity in the next room. Everyone left alive in the valley who was not fighting had fled but my mother had been too pregnant to leave. She would not have left even if she could have; she believed it was better to die in your home than on the run.

I have often thought of that.

It is more than twenty years since and I still wake with a start to the smell of snow, the echoes of gunfire across the valley. But these memories from my childhood are just out of reach and slippery somehow, like a bright fish flashing through my hands.

My world was small. It could be walked across in one morning. I remember it now in pieces. The bright sky snaked like a rope above us between the ice-topped mountains rising on every side. The sun would appear in the morning from behind the mountain peaks in the east and sweep over the valley, touching our house and then disappear behind another mountain peak west of the valley. A brief moment of brightness in the deep shadow.

I remember the sound of my mother praying as the light started across the valley. I would hear her whispering in the darkness, as the animals stirred and grumbled in the next room. *Subhanallah, Alhamdolillah* . . .

I remember the belligerent call of our long-legged rooster. I remember the smell of smoke as she started a fire for breakfast. The bright orange of the cornbread. The black tea. The pure white of the goat's milk. I remember her hands. Her mouth. The lines around her eyes. My memories of her are never still. She is always moving. Showing my sister, Farrukh, how to do something. Stopping to touch the back of my head.

And I remember the feeling that there was never any problem that she could not solve. That she was the strongest and bravest. She refused to hide. 'God is kind,' she would whisper. 'Everything will be all right.'

As she fed the animals, fetched water and swept the house, I would help her, asking questions: why was the sky blue, did the animals dream and what was beyond the mountains surrounding our house?

And I asked her why my father was not a real person with eyes, and arms, and a body, but just a photo in a rusting metal frame. A man with a thick black beard, wearing a grey hat, looking back at us so seriously. Sometimes someone would come to the house and ask where my father was, if he was there, and I would point at that photo on the wall. Sometimes their smiles would confuse me, but as time passed on, it didn't bother me so much. Sometimes my mother would tell me how tall he was, how he would ride on a huge white horse, up and down the valley, giving instructions to his farmers and labourers, before the war. She would tell me stories about my older brothers, Amin and Asad, and dad's second wife and her children who had fled the fighting one hot summer. She would tell me how they left in the dark. How she wished it had been light so she could have seen the faces of her sons one more time. I would often think about them.

I knew that out beyond our valley there was a whole land of mountains, valleys and plains. There were people who were not like us, people who for more than a hundred years had wanted to kill us and control the land, who would come from behind the mountain, up the valley every summer. They would kill men and women; the children would disappear forever.

But that felt far away in the winter. The whole valley would choke with snow and ice.

Sometimes our neighbour Jafar would come with his son Tariq to help clear snow, or help with a sick animal, but months could pass without seeing anyone – it was just me, my mother, my sisters Farrukh and Taj, our hens, our goats and sheep, the two red bulls with their curved horns, our white donkey and our noisy rooster.

In the spring, the white mountains would turn into a beautiful garden growing among the rocks: almond, apricot and mulberry trees flowering, the golden wheat in the fields either side of the river. These changes of seasons and scenery would bring a glimpse of both freedom and fear. Freedom from the harsh cold in the mountains and fear that fighting would break out again and the monsters with guns from behind the tall mountain would come and attack us again. As the plants grew green and the birds returned to the valley, so too did the sound of rocket-propelled grenades and machine-gun fire.

When it was warm enough, I would sit outside and play with rocks. I would graze the animals in the mountains.

I would collect firewood. I would think about who made the trees, the rocks and the stars that shone down so brightly above the gorge. I would sit with my legs dangling down and listen to the sound of water running down the valley. I would wonder where the water had come from and where it was going. I wondered who made the monsters and their guns.

We would hear the sound of gunfire from down the valley, and we would run up the valley with the women and children crying. If the fire came from above us, we would run down the valley, wailing, praying and pleading. Sometimes we would stay for days or weeks and occasionally even months at a time in nearby villages, waiting for the fighting to quiet down or move somewhere else. Sometimes families from elsewhere in the valley would appear and stay in our valley.

At times, armed men appeared out of the mountains to slaughter our animals, holding their guns at my mother's head, asking 'Where is your husband, your sons?' One time she was not quick enough with her answer and they put their guns to the back of her head. I would close my eyes and cover my ears with my hands and pray for God to save my mother.

I couldn't look but I also needed to know if they would shoot her. At that moment there was gunfire across the valley and for a moment I thought they had fired the gun. It was as if all of the organs inside my body failed and I died a thousand times. But they hurried off across the valley. Later I learned that Farrukh and Taj had been hidden, watching too. When we were sure they had gone, we came running, crying to my mother. 'Everything will be all right,' she said. 'God is kind.'

One winter, when the fighting stopped, my mother brought some of the women in the village together to find a teacher who could teach the young children how to read and write.

Eventually, they found someone. I walked two miles down the icy valley to the Masjid for my first-ever lessons. I was excited to be doing something new but it was the most people together at once I would have ever seen and I was nervous. The Masjid was built from mud and stone, high over a clear stream.

The teacher was called an Akhund. He was a stooping, round old man with a grey beard down to his chest, and a neat white turban. He would open up his torn Qur'an and point at a page: 'Read this line, you *harami.*' When we struggled, he would just scream that we were 'sons of devils' louder. I remember one boy was so nervous, he peed himself, while the other boys laughed and pointed.

The Akhund dragged the boy down to the floor, slapping and kicking at him, then twisting his cold-reddened ears between his fat, wrinkled fingers. The terrified boy's face turned first red, then pale, tears streaming down his face, crying in the silence of his own voice. Then the Akhund asked some of the boys who were laughing to take it in turns to slap his face.

He said we did not deserve his teaching. None of us. That there had been no one to teach him when he was our age. That we were lucky. It had been a crime to get an education when he was our age. He told us that the monsters had mas-sacred our people, stolen our lands, kidnapped our women and children because we were different and that we belonged to Hazara people. He had looked at us and repeated. Little children. I remember the beard around his crooked, stained teeth made me think of a cat's mouth.

I did not understand who he was talking about but I under-stood the look on his face, of anger and also of pain.

Why would someone stop children from going to school? Why would they take the children away from their homes?

That night, I tried to tell my mother but she only shushed me, and told me I must work hard and do what the Akhund told me and focus on my lessons. I fell asleep in the shadows to her stroking my hair.

A couple of months later, I got sick for the rest of the winter. I would suddenly faint without any obvious reasons. My Mother thought it was the Akhund's evil eye that had made me sick because he had told her a couple of times that he just couldn't believe how fast I was learning everything he taught. These random and basic literacy classes only happened a few winters before I no longer saw the Akhund. I do not know what happened to him. Although, the Akhund had gone, my curiosity about the world around me kept growing and growing. So, I would often follow my Mother around the house asking her endless questions. Sometimes she would answer me. Other times she wouldn't. Either way, I was not satisfied. When I got a little older, maybe around seven or eight years old, I came across a pile of old books with torn and yellowed pages abandoned on the shelves covered in dust next to the barn. I was trying to teach myself how to read them. One winter when my Mother couldn't find a teacher for us, the children in the village, I begged her to buy me a pen anyway. She bought me one pen after I really, really insisted. But there was no paper. Those things were in very short supply. So, after some hard thinking, I found an A-4 sized piece of cardboard and attached a piece of clean plastic over it. It served as a whiteboard for the entire winter. I would copy the words from the torn yellow pages onto my new plastic whiteboard again and again until I learned how to read and write some basic words.

Grandma lived a few miles down the valley with her other grandchildren. We would see her only occasionally when she would climb up the rocky valley with her walking stick to visit. And sometimes, only sometimes when we really, really insisted, she would tell us stories. She would tuck us under the goat wool blanket and, her wrinkled face lit almost purple by firelight, she would whisper stories. The ones we liked best were the stories about monsters . . .

The one-eyed witch attacked young mothers while they were giving birth and removed their hearts to feast upon. People claimed that they had seen her drinking blood from a young mother who had died giving birth. Or the huge monster with massive eyes, a long nose and sharp claws, who attacked villages, snatching little children from the arms of their parents and disappearing forever. No one would ever hear anything from them ever again. To ask after them was to risk more attacks. So, everyone would remain silent, bury their pain inside their bellies and carry on. Later, I found out that while the first story was probably fiction, the second had actually happened.

She told us stories of the castles, the great feasts there had been. How the men butchered goats, sheep and chickens and the women cooked rice, lamb, goat and chicken. Then they would all sing and dance together. There were stories of people and families getting together singing and celebrating but I had never witnessed one myself to believe it. I could not imagine where this would be allowed. It all seemed strange, like a story from another world.

'Good things never last long,' whispered Grandma through her missing front teeth, taking another long slow sip of her tea. As she told her stories, I felt the hairs on my arms rise up.

She told us one particular story of a girl called Shereen Begum, who tried to raise an army against a monstrous king called King Abdulrahman Khan, who attacked and massacred our people, the Hazara. He killed the men and kidnapped the women and children, up and down the villages, valleys and mountains all over the country. How Shereen rode her white horse up and down the valleys, calling on all girls to come out and defend their homes. At first, everyone ignored her, but she would not give up. She continued galloping on her horse across the valleys, calling out to all girls to join her and fight with dignity against the blood-sucking monsters, attacking them. Her voice was nearly drowned out by the sound of the approaching armies.

But finally, one of her best friends came out to join her. Then another, and another, and another – until their numbers reached hundreds. She took them to the castle, armed them and trained them as best she could. Then they rode out, through the ravaged land, which had become slick with blood, the field and gardens full of bodies. Finally, they realised that tens of thousands of highly trained armies of monsters were rapidly closing in on them from all directions. The girls fought like lionesses, killing scores of armed soldiers up and down the valley. But after many hours of intense battle, they were left with no choice but to retreat into the nearby mountains. They continued battling with thousands of heavily armed soldiers across the valleys, villages and mountains to their last bullets. When they ran out of ammunition, they threw stones, until there were only forty girls left, surrounded by the enemy with their backs to a steep cliff face. And as the monsters closed in, they jumped, and as they fell, their colourful long skirts and scarves hung like beautiful butterflies.

'Did they die, Grandma?' Farrukh asked as she jumped up and sat next to Grandma, her eyes wide.

'Nooo, no, my dear child, they did not die,' Grandma muttered as she ran her fingers through my sister's hair. 'No, they did not die. They all flew to heaven like flying angels. That's what they did – flew to heaven like flying angels.' I did not understand what she meant by *flying angel* but for a moment, I imagined a group of young village girls in their beautiful and colourful dresses, like butterflies rising into the sky and over the mountains above our valley.

'Be like those girls, my dear. And never let monsters take you away. Always be brave, fight back, and never, ever let monsters take you away.' It was already past bedtime; Grandma pulled the blanket over the three of us near the cooling-down *tandoor*, before blowing out the candle next to her. That was my understanding of the world as a child. There was the valley and there were armed monsters who would always come.

For a brief period, it seemed as if the fighting had slowed down, at least in and around our valley. The constant thunder of machine guns and rocket-propelled grenades breaking the deep silence of a dark night far enough away to allow the villagers to go about their lives with a little more ease and comfort. Some people who had fled their homes began coming back in the hope of living peacefully with their families in the village. My father too turned up from several years of exile in neighbouring countries. However, what no one would've ever imagined was that such a moment of relative peace was just a rare moment of calm before a terrifying storm.

And one day, new monsters came. Much more frightening and brutal than the existing ones.

There had been rumours for some time about the birth of a new type of monster. Some would report them as an army of zombies, covered in white *kafan* and large turbans while heavily armed with blood-dripping machetes and machine guns, attacking people in the mountain villages. Others would describe them as monsters covered in black from head to toe,

faces concealed beyond unusually long hair, beards and turbans, their bloodied huge eyes staring from behind thick, black
fabric with Kalashnikovs in their hawked claws. Some of them
had bombs strapped to their chests and sometimes the male
monsters would wear *burqas* to better deliver death.

These new monsters, which some said were called the
Talib or Taliban, moved quickly, killing everyone – the old,
the women, the children. People in the village whispered that
they would destroy everything – musical instruments and tel-
evisions, statues and buildings. Some thought they were the
end of the world – God's punishment for the sins of our years
of fighting, but some said they were here to finally bring peace.

Rumours and speculation circulated in silent whispers up
and down the valley. There were stories of their great victories,
of warlords who had defeated the great invaders now suddenly
falling overnight to these new enemies. There were many
different types of monsters. They were all divided into groups.
Each one had a different name and fiercely fought one another
over power and territory. But they all, called themselves Mujahideen and shouted Allahu Akbar before killing innocent men,
women and children.

The villagers gathered around their worn-out radios to
learn of the news, as the new monsters spread like a virus and
rapidly captured more and more territories, as the cities fell to
them. And soon no one said they were angels sent to create
peace and justice. Now there were just the stories of massacres,
of them killing people like those in our valley. Because we
looked different, and we worshipped a different god. We said
the wrong sort of prayers, we had the wrong sort of mullahs.
We were now the infidels who must be wiped out. Again.

One dry summer night, when clusters of stars were bright
in the sky over the darkness of the valley, a loud voice burst

out from the radio. It told of the death of infidels in a city not far from us. With God's help they had killed them all, then a large crowd of violent voices exploded in celebration: 'ALLAHU AKBAR, ALLAHU AKBAR . . .' God is great, God is great. The man announced that all minority ethnic groups must leave Afghanistan and go to other countries, but the voice said that the Hazaras had nowhere to run to. 'You are surrounded. Even if you fly up to the sky, we will pull you by the foot and if you hide in the ground, we will pull you by the hair. You have nowhere to go but to the grave.'

In the coming months, there would be more stories of them bursting into cities across the country, shooting to the left and right, killing anything that moved – shopkeepers, cart pullers, mothers and their babies. They did not spare the goats and donkeys. They massacred thousands of innocent women and children, as well as men, then searched house to house for the remaining infidel families. It was said that they needed to kill enough of us to enter paradise. The adults whispered and moaned. The monsters shot anything that moved, some-times even each other in their eagerness to kill us. Some men, including my father, once again disappeared from the village. My Mother said they had gone to defend us against the invad-ing monsters. Others, fled the village altogether, searching for shelter elsewhere, leaving behind women and children. But my Mother's motto was still the same: *its more dignified to die at home than on the run.*

Out of that dusty silver box came voices telling of more death. Across the country, city after city fell. I thought back to my grandmother's stories, of the monsters coming closer. The few remaining men disappeared from the village. We would sit and try to eat as we listened, but we had no appetite with so much death.

14

'Try and have something to eat,' my mother would whisper, stroking my head. *'God is kind. I wonder how God can be kind and let such evil happen.'*

I would look across to the high northern mountains still covered in snow, bright against the belly of the sky. If the monsters came with their guns from those mountains, what would I do? Would I have the strength to fight like Shereen?

There were rumours that they were starving us out of the mountains, stopping anything from getting to us but that year, Mother had collected vegetables from our farms and nearby mountains to go with the little corn and wheat the fields had produced. We were in the middle of a drought and there was not enough food. Struggling families began abandoning their children and babies on the streets or in bushes, hoping other families from the neighbouring villages who had food might pick them up and feed them. There were whispered conversations about the smugglers, men who could get you away to safety. The last men and older boys left the valley.

One hot summer's day, my mother brought home a severely malnourished, starving little girl. She said her name was Ruqiya, and that she was nine years old, but her arms and legs looked more like she was four. Mother found her half unconscious left in a dried-out riverbed under a drying mulberry tree. At first, Mother fed her drops of goat's milk into her dry mouth, and she gradually recovered and became a healthy young girl.

There was no medicine and that, plus the lack of food, meant that everyone was getting sick. Mother had a couple of packs of small, yellow-looking painkillers called *konaine*. They were wrapped in many folds and secretly kept deep inside a locked box for *a bad day*, she would say, but whenever desperate women and children from neighbouring valleys and villages came, asking for just one painkiller, she would give it to them in the hope it would help their dying patients.

We were the richest family in the valley and my mother felt it was our responsibility to help the poorest families up and down the village. High in the valley, many families survived only on foraged plants and their legs stopped working. They pulled themselves down the valley by their hands, their legs dragging behind them.

One night, the radio brought the news that the last resistance stronghold had fallen. There was nothing stopping the monsters flooding into our valley.

As the sun set, I began to feel an unbearable weight on my chest, so that I could hardly breathe. My dry tongue would run into silent prayers in my bitter-tasting mouth, reciting one verse from Qur'an after another, in the hope that these verses would have the power to keep the monsters away during the night. It was as if the clear mountain air had been tainted with fear and despair, rising up from below us.

Though we knew there was nowhere we could go where we would be safe, many families left everything behind and ran for their lives, including our neighbours. They criss-crossed into other valleys, hoping they might escape to there.

One night, when I was thirteen years old, my mother woke me and told me to put on warm clothes. She handed me a bag. She said I needed to go with the men outside, to the next valley, where it would be safe. I would be with our neighbours, just for a little while. I was still half asleep. She touched the back of my head. 'Justice will return. God is kind.'

It was not until a couple of hours later, as we trudged under the stars, that I realised my mother was not walking with us.

2

Afghanistan

Every time the truck jolted, silent whispers and prayers would burst out: *Biiiiismillah! Ya Allah, help us*. It was the only sound you could hear above the sound of the battered truck's engine, as it dragged itself up and down the steep mountain roads in the darkness.

Opposite me, our former neighbour Jafar, his son Tariq, and his son-in-law Karim sat, staring straight ahead of them. I recognised a few people from the valley but there were many people I didn't recognise. We waited in the next valley for a few days but it was not safe. I asked about my mother, but Jafar told me I was to go with them. Farrukh and Taj were to stay with my mother. It had been arranged. So, we got in the truck again.

Inside, children, men and women were packed tightly in with each other. There was no chatting. Sometimes a parent would shush a grumbling child. In the moonlight, I watched a child asleep in his father's lap, and tried to ignore the ghost of my mother's hand on the back of my head. As the truck moved slowly away from my valley, it became harder and harder. All I could think about was that the further this truck took me from home, the harder it would be for my Mother to find me and for me to find my way back to her. As quickly as these thoughts would appear, I'd find myself trying to deny

17

their existence. Every now and then we would stop for people to rush behind rocks to relieve themselves.

After a couple of days, the truck stopped in the semi-darkness at the end of a long day. The sky was streaked dusty pink and purple. Around us were hills and a handful of lopsided huts. There were fields with half-dead stalks, abandoned to die.

I was clinging onto a thin line of rope, wrapped around some bags of dried fruit, with my legs dangling over the rusted back of the vehicle. I could see a few men on the driver's side of the truck muttering to one another, the shadows of their heads moving in the light from the rising moon. I could hear whispering from some women closer by; one of them said that the truck driver was refusing to go any further, that it was too dangerous because we were too close to Kandi Posht. Kandi Posht was in the Shah-Joy district, the only crossing point into the outside world. It was famous as a place where fleeing Hazaras were dragged out of their vehicles, killed and dumped at the roadside. One of the others saw me listening and motioned for the woman to be quiet.

My entire body shivered; my skin felt like it was being poked with needles.

I had heard countless stories about this place. Kandi Posht, where the monsters had been blockading our region for years, starving us of food and medicine, as they competed to get into heaven by killing us. This was the most notorious of the slaughter districts, where many thousands of us had been killed and left in the desert. 'Grave is the only place where the Hazaras must go,' they had announced on the radio but they didn't even bother burying the dead bodies. They would just dump them on the side of the road for the dogs to eat.

After a few minutes, the passenger side door opened and then there was a voice.

'We cannot continue any further. It is too dangerous. We will keep you updated. But for now, get off the truck, everyone.'

The whispering got louder as the people on the truck realised what was happening. Some were whispering under their breaths: 'They are not good, *rah-Balad*.' Smugglers. The door shut and people stayed where they were, agitated.

After a few moments the door opened again, this time the door banging loudly with the force.

'I told you all to get the fuck off the truck now. Why are you still here? GET OFF NOW!' People began to grab their belongings – clothes, old blankets, bags of dried fruit, and hurry down from the truck. As soon as everyone was off, the truck roared into the darkness.

No one spoke. Everyone just sat at the edge of the dusty road for the night. I had my thickest winter coat on and tried to sleep, arms wrapped around my knees and curled up on the hard ground. Babies cried throughout the night, cold and hungry, but their exhausted mothers were too tired to comfort them.

'Wake up, *o bacha'* boy.' I recognised Jafar's voice and opened my eyes. The sky was just lightening with dawn. He was murmuring to Tariq and Karim.

'We need to find shelter nearby for when the smugglers come to find us.'

I heard Karim's voice. 'Will they come?'

'They must do.'

Tariq and Karim were gone for hours and came back late in the afternoon, reporting back that they went from hut to hut but could not find any place to stay – everywhere was shut or abandoned. 'Not even a mosque or something?' Jafar demanded, his voice containing a hint of both anger and disapproval.

'No,' the young men responded, looking down at their feet in fear and respect.

Jafar stood up suddenly and walked away, his back stooped, his head leaning forward deep in thought. Minutes later, he reappeared and told everyone to pack up and follow him. We followed him along a narrow dirt pathway, then dry riverbeds under yellow-leaved trees, before arriving at an abandoned mosque surrounded by rotting trees.

There was an odd smell that made me feel on edge.

The thick mud-walls of the mosque were torn up by bullets, leaving sand that was stained red. The door hung rotten from the doorframe. Wild grass had grown in front of the door and the tiny broken window was choked with thick spiderwebs. I felt the hairs on my arm rise.

Jafar pushed the door and there was the sound of something breaking but the door hardly moved. He pushed again, harder and harder, until it finally gave in and collapsed back into the mosque, releasing a cloud of dust. There was grass growing from the walls and dirty rugs scattered on the floor. There was a rush of movement as whatever was living there scampered into the dark corners of the room.

Jafar instructed the women to sweep the floor and put the few scruffy mattresses on top of the scattered carpets on the wet floor. It was just before dusk when Jafar told the boys to go around the village and knock on the doors to see if anyone was still alive. We needed warm milk and bread for the little ones.

We divided ourselves into groups of two and walked in different directions through the uneasy silence of the houses. I followed Tariq, watching his broad shoulders as I walked behind him. We walked from one abandoned house to another, quietly knocking on doors, but there was no response. By the time we reached the last of the huts, it was already dark but then there was a small hut just visible in the distance, further up into the hills. After crashing through bushes, tripping over tree branches and the rocks in the dried-out riverbed, we made it to the hut, which sat on a small hill rising between two riverbeds. The mountain rose dark above us. Tariq knocked on the door. I wanted to get back to the others – we'd been away longer than we'd expected and it was getting dark.

'Tariq, I don't think there's anyone inside. Let's go back, it's too late,' I whispered. I wasn't sure if he had heard me. He mumbled something under his breath, which I couldn't hear, then knocked harder, making the door squeak. I sensed movement behind the door, then the sound of a gun clicking

'Don't move,' said a hoarse voice from somewhere behind the door.

We both froze. My mind went blank, standing in the darkness, my hands held up high over my head.

'What do you want? Do not lie to me and do not move!' barked the man. In the silence I thought I could hear the sound of his finger tightening on the trigger. My whole body was tense and I had a pain in my stomach, as if I might vomit. I wanted my mother here to tell me what to do.

'Please don't shoot us,' Tariq begged. 'We are only looking for some milk or bread for the sick children.'

After a few more moments of deafening silence, the man cleared his throat. 'Listen *bachem*, it's too dangerous to be out at this time of night. You should go back immediately to wherever you're staying and stay there,' the man's voice trembled.

Tariq and I rushed back, hurdling the bushes and branches and rocks. With every noise, I imagined the sound of a gun firing, echoing through the dead village. We stopped when we were far enough away and leant our hands on our knees, panting. Tariq laughed in relief and for a moment he looked young again.

By the time we made it back to the abandoned mosque, the women and children had fallen asleep where they sat. A fire had died down, leaving behind a tiny red glow among the ashes.

'Boys, what took you so long? Did you bring anything?' Jafar demanded. His voice shook with barely suppressed anger.

Tariq looked at me for a moment then briefly explained: 'We went everywhere, door to door, but no one answered.' He did not mention the man in the hut. Jafar, who was leaning on his right elbow, near the dying fire, pointed to the furthest corner of the mosque. 'There, find a place to sleep,' he told me. I found a spot, right at the edge, on the side of the door, wrapped myself inside my jacket, curled up and slept on the wet floor. I was asleep in minutes.

It was a night of bad dreams, where shadowy creatures came towards me in the darkness, their long fingers reaching out for me. I tried to shout out for help, but my mouth would not open, my body would not move, as if there was a great weight on top of me. I could hardly breathe. I slipped in and out of the nightmares, unable to tell what was real. I lay there sweating in the darkness, listening to the sound of snoring and babies sobbing, hoping for dawn.

'*Allahu Akbar*,' I heard Jafar reciting his morning prayer. *Allahu Akbar*. I was so glad to listen to his calming voice in the dark before dawn. Soon after, everyone rushed out to prepare for morning *Namaaz*.

That morning, the men gathered and discussed what to do. Some felt it was a bad place and we should leave. Some thought it would be better to split up, be easier to hide family by family. Some thought that it was safer to stick together. Nobody seemed to know if the smugglers would still come. These men knew there was money in it for them, but we simply didn't know if it was too dangerous to stay. Some left to find their own way, some went back the way we had come, went others on towards the city, but many of us remained in the mosque. I wanted us to do whatever meant my Mother would be able to find me.

Days passed in the mosque, but we heard no news of the smugglers. We walked for hours to find what little food we could, pulling the plants from the abandoned fields and mixing it with the tiny amounts of grain and dried fruit we had left. We walked down to the riverbed to fill our bottle from a spring that did not appear tainted. I thought of my mother's orange cornbread, the pure white of a cup of goat's milk.

Jafar finally sent Tariq and Karim to search for information about the security situation in the neighbouring villages and the whereabouts of smugglers. They returned tired and downhearted, bringing news of how the monsters had installed checkpoints in and around the city to identify and shoot infidels. How there were rumours that these men were disguising themselves as smugglers, first agreeing to take people to safety before dumping their bodies in the dried-out riverbeds.

As the days passed, our hopelessness grew. People began to get sick. The children and elders had permanent diarrhoea and fevers were spreading through the group. My whole body was covered in pink bites from insects that lived in the damp earth where I slept. They itched permanently and spread until they covered my entire body. I had a fever and dizziness. I could hardly force down the small amount of food we had.

Ishaq Reza, a short, grey-haired man with a curved back I recognised from down the valley, was very sick. I would hear him groaning all through the day and night.

The women were not eating enough food to produce milk for their babies. The children and babies cried constantly from a mixture of hunger, illness and fear. The constant talk of the monsters ensured that every noise was them bursting in.

Ishaq Reza's health began to deteriorate further, hour by hour and even minute by minute, until he was slipping in and out of consciousness. Tariq and Karim rushed out to find a mullah to read the *Kalima* in case he died during the night. Later that evening, they returned with an old man, named Hajji. After studying the patient, moving his hand up and down and looking at his sick face, he said, 'The man is suffering from some sort of cold or chest infection.' He watched as Ishaq Reza struggled to breathe.

He turned to Jafar and said, 'We used to have a *tabeeb*, a traditional doctor, in the nearby village. God bless him. He was found smuggling medicine from the city and was shot.' He paused, staring into the distance. 'Only God can help us, only God . . .' He repeated it as he stared at the dark corner of the mosque where I slept.

I thought I heard him mutter, 'This is where the dead were left for weeks, when there was no one left to bury them.'

Just before dawn, the old man recited the *Kalima*, before gently brushing his hands over Ishaq Reza's eyes and face a couple of times.

When it was light, Tariq, Karim and a few other elders buried him in the graveyard outside the mosque. Hajji, with his white turban wrapped around his head, read out the *Fatiha*, a verse from the Qur'an, after the burial ceremony. I helped to shovel soil onto his grave but I could barely hold the handle; the insect bites had made my hands severely swollen and I was shivering constantly. Like the others, I also had diarrhoea and fever. We sat, too weak to do anything but wait for the smugglers to arrive, or for the monsters to come and put us out of our misery. I drifted in and out of sleep, sometimes it was light outside, sometimes dark.

At some point, men wearing dark headscarves burst in, ordering us up. We were so weak, we limped onto a small truck. Jafar tried to ask them who they were but they just shouted: 'Up, Up!' The nervous sounds of prayers whispered under everyone's breath could be heard as the truck started moving. They were taking us to be slaughtered. They would dump our bodies in riverbeds. We climbed up into a metal box on the back of the truck and the door clanged shut behind us, the sound of heavy bolts drawing across. There was nothing to sit on, or hold onto, just the bare walls of metal.

I cannot breathe. I cannot live. There was no air in the truck. There was no light. I wanted to inhale all the air in the world, to fill my deflated lungs, to keep my heart pumping, to be able to keep going for a little longer. I wanted to shout out, but there was no breath left in my lungs to push the words out and no one out there to help me if I did. It was as if my lungs, heart, and the rest of my organs were no longer connected. They were giving up. All I could manage was a strangled croak, like the sound of a goat under the butcher's knife. We tumbled over the rough roads, sure that every minute was taking us closer to our deaths; that soon, the door would open and men with guns or knives would burst in, their faces bright with thoughts of heaven.

We bounced into each other, weak and afraid.

My eyes stung like someone had peeled my eyelids back and rubbed them with green pepper. My nose felt like it had been caught up in burning coal fire, my throat as if it was being turned inside out. I lost all track of time. I wondered if someone would bury me like we buried Ishaq Reza.

I woke to a strangled voice.

'We're stopping.'

Another screech from another corner. 'Yes, we're stopping, Yes, it's stopping. Thank God, it's stopping.' They were right. The truck was slowing down and came to a stop. The door opened, letting in a glorious cool breeze. The fresh air expanded in my depraved lungs and injected a glimpse of life and hope amid chaos. Immediately, everyone rushed out. I was the last one to get to the door. A tall, giant black figure in the dark, head covered with a black turban and wrapped around his head and face, grabbed me by the wrist and threw me onto the ground. Was this the moment the bullet would come? I turned my face up to the light, squinting, shaking.

3

Iran/Turkey Border

We were running in the darkness, my heart pounding, the sound of my breath rasping in my chest, trying not to disturb rocks as we moved closer to the crossing point between Iran and Turkey. We knew that there were no rules; soldiers on both sides were free to shoot anyone trying to cross the border. I was moving as carefully and deftly as possible when there was the thunderous noise of machine-gun fire in front of us. The bullets buzzed all around us, throwing up stones and dust. As one, we turned and ran, without thinking about a direction, all of us trying to get away from the terrifying noise. We were like a herd of sheep scrabbling to get over each other to escape from the predator. I was searching for shelter, anything – rocks, bushes, the flesh of someone else. I changed direction and began to run uphill, away from everyone else. I stopped and crouched behind a boulder, trying to get some air into my lungs. But I heard the sound of a tank crushing rocks under its chains; it sounded as if it were right behind me. It was a noise I had never heard in my life just two days before and now I would recognise it anywhere. I glanced around the boulder but couldn't see anything in the darkness; all I could hear was the sound of those rocks under the rolling chains echoing across the hills. I was completely disoriented. As I started to move, from the side of me, which I thought was a steep-sided riverbed, I heard gunfire.

I turned back and ran in the opposite direction, bullets spraying into the ground where I had been. I just kept running downhill, tripping on rocks and stones, my feet sliding on the loose ground. I lost my footing jumping over a larger rock and slid down on my back, colliding with something in the darkness, rolling along with a whole load of dry soil, dirt and stones before coming to a stop in a bruised heap. I tried to get up but retched from a pain in my side, heaving into the dirt. I pulled myself along by my arms, just like those poor people from up the valley. I dragged myself to a larger boulder and lay still. Above me, I heard the sounds of trucks and tanks' engines, people shouting and the sound of gunfire. Gradually the sounds receded and there was a deafening silence as if nothing had ever happened. The wind blew, and as my heart began to slow, I became aware of the pain throughout my body. I could feel a constant stream of warm blood running down my cheek and a sharp urgent pain in my thigh. I didn't want to check too closely in case I had been shot, so I lay there, hoping it might disappear. Time stretched like a piece of elastic, while I lay panting.

I wondered if Reza, my friend, had made it and hoped he had. I remembered when I had arrived at the concrete cattle house at the base of this mountain – it must have been a month before, after weeks of being driven in the metal boxes of trucks through Pakistan and Iran. Harsh metal walls of trucks was all I'd seen for a long time. Every now and then water and very little food was passed in, but it was still much more than we'd had at the mosque. Jafar, Tariq and Karim and I had filled our shrunken stomachs.

On those long drives where the hours felt like years, we continued our journey on. The man who had grabbed me by the wrist and pulled me to the ground after we were rounded up at the mosque and put on a truck was a smuggler. But instead of meeting our end, we were set on our journey again, further and further away from Mother. The hours on the truck were broken up by the sound of gunfire and the truck speeding up, being forced out to face police officers who would demand money, and the smugglers stopping and beating people at random with sticks and guns' butts and barrels. At one of these stops, I was separated from Jafar, Tariq and Karim and never saw them again. No one in my truck knew their name. I spent the rest of the journey with people from far away, who spoke a strange dialect. There was no way of getting a message to my mother now. No way of her finding me. Every minute had taken me further away from everything I knew, from Farrukh, and Taj. When we finally arrived at the next stop, it was Reza who came striding over to me, grinning. He greeted me in our familiar dialect and took me to sit with a group of other Hazara boys.

'We have to stick together,' he had said, handing me a bowl. I told him I wanted to get back to my mother and sister, to my home, but he shook his head. 'The monsters will kill you, my friend,' he said. 'There is nothing for us back there.'

I guessed Reza was a few years older than me, but he had survived so much. The smuggler, a middle-aged man with a long, curved nose and a sharp goatee on his pointy face, had kept changing the date for the crossing. As we waited, bored in that tiny concrete box, we kept each other entertained. We played cards and told jokes and sometimes stories. One night Reza told his story, how he had survived two massacres, the massacre at Afshar and one at Mazar-i-Sharif, five years apart. The first time, while the bullets and grenades had slammed into their hut, he had managed to survive with his sister and mother by making a hole in the wall and running from street corner to street corner, somehow avoiding the bullets raining down on them. That night, tens of thousands were not so lucky and died.

The monsters searched through the rubble for survivors, women, men and children calling out for help. They would drag them free, then rape and torture them, before slitting their throats in celebration.

Reza and his mother and sister travelled to the city of Mazar-i-Sharif that was considered safer and for a few years it was, before monsters arrived there too. Until they were woken by the sounds of machine-gun fire again, as hundreds of white SUVs drove up and down the streets, firing at everything that moved. Again, they ran, this time to Iran, on their way to Turkey. Here they became separated and Reza was arrested by police and badly beaten. He had been deported back and forth between countries for months before finally winding up with a group looking to cross into Turkey. Our little cowshed gang had started the crossing together but once the shooting started, we fled and I didn't see what happened to anyone.

Lying in that riverbed, I still couldn't see or hear anything but avoided moving or making any sound in case it alerted the soldiers who might be hiding somewhere nearby. As I cooled down, my body revealed new aches. I realised I would have to check myself properly if I wanted to survive. I brushed the dirt from my hands as best as I could, then reached for my head.

Slowly, over a few minutes, I felt around the wound, trying to feel if it was a bullet hole. I almost laughed with relief when I realised it wasn't. I stood up, testing my weight on my thigh and though it hurt, I was able to put weight on it. *Perhaps I might not die alone in this riverbed.*

Gradually, I started limping up the steep riverbed. Every few paces I would slip back down on the loose stones, but little by little I made it. I stopped every few minutes to crouch down and listen. I imagined my ears pointing upwards like a frightened rabbit. No engines, no footsteps.

What happened to the tanks and soldiers, the shooting? What happened to Reza, and the rest of the boys – and the rest of the crew?

I started dragging my leg after me in the dark, sideways up and down across the many hills, towards a bunch of scattered, fading lights buried behind some distant hills and mountains, far away. I only hoped I was moving in the right direction. After climbing up and down a couple of hills, I began to hear some thin whispers, and gentle movements somewhere out ahead of me. Then there were scattered footsteps, people reluctantly coming out of their little hiding trenches from up and down the silent hills. Soon, everyone, hundreds of people, started walking in the same direction, towards the small villages at the base of the mountain. I continued dragging my injured right leg. One hand on the right thigh and the other one on the side of my head. By the time we were about to approach the little village, the sky above the mountain in the east had already begun lightening with the dawn.

Then there was a voice.

'Don't move,' several nervous voices suddenly started barking in heavily accented Farsi that I could barely understand. 'Sit down, don't move.' It was a group of armed men, heads wrapped up with lined scarfs and their guns rattling in their trembling hands. Kneeling with our heads down, our hands raised in the air, we waited for the moment the rattling would become firing. I kept my eyes shut, hands over my head. Many voices of men continued barking from somewhere above my head. I squinted and from the corner of my eye, I glimpsed men in baggy black tracksuits, old jackets, with lined, dusted headscarves wrapped around their heads. *They do not look like soldiers or police officers. So, who are they?* I wondered.

They swung their guns nervously at us, their fingers on the triggers. I buried my head further down in front of me, avoiding eye contact. Then they began to poke and push us, shouting: 'Move!' We shuffled along the path, gradually moving up into the foothills of the mountain. Sometimes they would stop and come round to everyone, poke guns into their sides and say: 'Money!' Some people reached into their clothes and produced what they were asked for but many simply lifted their hands up to show empty palms. Sometimes the men slapped them for having nothing to offer. My heart filled when I caught sight of Reza knelt off to the side and he caught my eye, nodding quickly.

When the men were satisfied that no one had any more money left on them, they asked people one by one for the name of their smuggler. We were divided into groups, and they said they would call the smugglers and get them to pay for us. We listened to what sounded like an exchange of threats for hours and I was worried that there would be a gun battle.

Every time I attempted to shift position or touch the wounds and bruises over my head and thigh, the gunmen would bark something, poking me with the end of their guns and threatening to shoot if I moved again. After hours of constant torture and death threats, a deal was apparently made between the smugglers, and they agreed to hand us over by midnight.

The smugglers, a group of armed men, arrived by midnight and marched us a little way off the path, then opened a padlocked metal door and pushed us all down into the darkness. It quickly became clear we were in some sort of underground barn. I smelt the familiar stink of sheep shit. I rushed up to Reza, who was standing with his friend Anwar and the other boys, and we touched fists.

ACROSS MOUNTAINS, LAND AND SEA

'We're all alive,' said Anwar, grinning.

'And now we are in shit again,' said Reza, smiling grimly. 'At least it is sheep shit this time, not cow shit.'

We found a spot at the far end of the barn and lay on a blanket of fresh sheep shit. The smell reminded me of the animals back home and as I drifted off to sleep, I imagined lying, listening to the sound of my siblings and mother breathing and the animals moving in the next room.

I dreamed that my nose and throat were blocked with something that I could not claw away, a weight pushing down on my throat, stopping me breathing.

I woke lying in fresh snow outside the barn, gasping. Bodies were dumped all around me. The smugglers had closed all of the vents of the barn as they were worried police could see in and so there was no air left in the barn. It was Reza who had sensed the poisonous gas inside before he lost consciousness. He had climbed over dozens of unconscious bodies out of the barn into the dark to find help. He had found the smugglers busy smoking opium in a warm and well-maintained guest room, not too far away, and he persuaded them to come and rescue the suffocating people. After that first night, they kept the vents open. We got into a routine, hiding during the day and then at the darkest hour of the night, the smugglers would lead us toward the border, and we would walk, run and sprint towards the crossing point in the darkness. But each time we'd be spotted and fired at by the border forces, like the first night. Then we had to run back to the village and the barn.

This happened four or five times until one night there was a miracle.

'Tonight, we will take you via a different route, a better route that the soldiers cannot guard during snowfall at night,' one of the armed men covered in black from head to toe announced, standing on a rock. He sounded more positive, unlike on previous nights, which had ended in miserable failure. 'We will get through tonight, *inshallah,*' Reza whispered as he continued listening to the announcement. Other groups nearby too would mumble, discussing things quietly, perhaps praying or cautiously celebrating the positive news among themselves.

While I did not have the faintest idea of what it would be like on the other side of the border if we did manage to get through, somehow deep down, I felt a little sense of excitement and hope, thinking it would have to be better than this. The air was thin and burning with cold on this mountain. And we were spending our nights sprinting and our days locked up in the dark.

'However, there is something we have to tell you,' he continued, 'The route we are going to take you through tonight is a minefield so you will need to be very careful.' The quiet, happy whispers among the crowd suddenly stopped, turning into a deafening silence, then into increased disappointment and moaning. I could hear some people complaining among themselves that they would rather wait, and others were just silent, confused.

'Well, we are going. Whatever happens, happens,' Reza muttered, shifting his shoulders in the cold. The man cleared his throat.

'The only way to stay safe is to make sure you follow the footsteps of the person in front of you without side-stepping – not even by an inch – if you don't want to die.' He jumped down from the rock into the snow.

'Oh, one last thing – if the person in front of you gets blown up by a landmine, you must continue moving forward in the same line, regardless,' he concluded.

'Now, get moving,' the other armed men ordered.

The news of landmines quickly turned into a delaying competition between the different groups and nationalities, each trying to let another group take the lead and risk getting blown up first. The more the armed smugglers insisted, the more everyone resisted moving forward – to the point where one of the smugglers activated his AK-47, threatening to shoot everyone if no one moved. But still, no one moved. Everyone remained static, immovable, as if they had all become like the surrounding rock, lifeless. It began to snow heavily. Amid the frightening silence, chaos and confusion, I heard Reza saying: 'Fuck it, let's go.' He stood up, shook off the snow piling up on his shoulders and took the lead. I followed him – so did everyone else, like a herd. I remembered at home during war or natural disasters no one in the valley would react until my mother took the lead. Then everyone followed her. I wished it was her leading me now.

Every time Reza lifted his feet from the fresh snow in front of me, I expected a sudden explosion, a thunderous sound to ricochet in my ears, inches away from me, blowing apart both Reza and me. I pictured our limbs flying up in the air among smoke and fire. I could feel my breath shortening and my heart pounding with every step, every foot lifted and placed as if it were a string attached to my pulse. I had already heard things about landmines and how they work, that they tend to explode when the foot on them is lifted, not when the foot is placed on them. I couldn't help wondering how I might survive the explosion if I happened to feel one beneath my feet.

'What if I throw myself sideways or lie down next to it and then lift my feet to minimise the damage? It might just take away one or both of my legs, leaving the upper body alive, at least,' Reza whispered back to me over his shoulder.

'At least there's no shit here.'

Between the snow, the mist and the darkness, it was near impossible to see anything right in front of me, let alone step exactly into the footprints ahead of me. The rocks were steep and slippery, and we were constantly walking at an angle. The ragged breathing of hundreds of exhausted, frightened people combined with the sounds of footsteps dragging through snow was horrifying. Several times, people lost their footing, exhausted, and slipped suddenly down the mountain, their cries quickly lost. We all just carried on, shuffling our way across the mountain, straining our ears for the click of a landmine as the snow fell in the darkness.

4

Turkey

A deep voice, in Turkish, said something urgent. About moving or stillness or both.

A pair of huge hands grabbed me by the back of my neck, choking me. Someone else cuffed me around the head, making me see bursts of light. Someone pulled a blindfold down over my eyes.

I tried to remove the fingers from my neck but they were like metal, unbending. In response they punched me low in the gut. Another, into my ribs, sending shocks through my body. My breath was driven out, I was a crumpled shell. I wanted to sit down but they dragged me on. I felt the light dim as I could feel myself fainting. But they kept lifting me, pulling me along.

They are taking me somewhere; they are taking me somewhere – where are they taking me? Are the monsters here too? Or were these the men who took children, who did things to them?

I cursed my stupidity. I had been walking back to the empty warehouse where Anwar and I were sleeping. Back from the 'job square' where men would come to find cheap labourers and cleaners.

I had just turned a corner and was about to cross the road when I'd caught movement out of the corner of my eye.

Then I was being pushed down some concrete steps into some sort of dark basement while being firmly held down on both sides. My feet dragged; I tried to shout but some hands choked me. At the bottom of the stairs, I landed on a concrete floor, and they let go but immediately launched a kick into my hip that knocked me forwards. I hit my head against something hard before falling onto something soft. It was a person, who immediately pushed me away from them, muttering: 'get the fuck off me'.

I sat up, seeing bars and a door in the dim light, just in time for Anwar to come flying in, landing on me and sending me backwards again. My delight at seeing him was abruptly removed by the pain that shot through my ribs as I fell back against the man in the cell again.

'I said move, little boy,' he said, shoving at me.

But I pushed back. 'You move,' I replied.

The cell door slammed shut behind us and I heard multiple locks shutting.

'They got you too,' said Anwar. I nodded.

He ran his tongue along the inside of his mouth, wincing and shaking his head.

'The fat one got me good.'

I was glad to see him. Anwar and I were among the very few people who had made it over the border crossing from Iran into Turkey that night. The rest had been caught and deported back.

In the shadows of the cell, I heard various voices murmuring and whispering inside the cell. I took a deep breath, inhaling the damp fetid air. It smelt of bad breath and cigarettes, fried onions and human shit. I heard a deep voice from the dark corner behind me.

'Where did they find you, little boy? We're all going to get deported . . . we're all going to get deported . . . we're going to get deported . . . ha-ha-ha.' The man winced and groaned.

I realised we had all received the same treatment. They must have gone around the city that morning rounding us up. Some remained quiet, some were praying quietly with dry mouths, others would call out from time to time. 'Officers, officers, please let us go – we have done nothing wrong. Please let us go,' they would plead until a voice called back. If they didn't quieten down, they would be struck on the arms through the bars with a baton, which made them jerk back. This would quieten them down for a little while, before the whining started up again. Over the next few hours, more and more people were flung into the cell and this time it was our turn to push them off us. There was so little room that fights would break out and the guards would burst in with their batons and fists and feet.

Anwar and I tried to move away from the doorway. But as soon as I shifted a little to my right or left to get closer to the concrete wall in the corner, someone would bark: 'Don't move!' The numbers of new people thrown into the cells gradually decreased as dusk fell. I wondered if they had got all of us – Kazim too. Or perhaps it was not his turn because he had lived in Iran. I thought of the English–Persian dictionary he had lent me. How we had tried those strange words in our mouths, saying them out loud to each other. Kazim had a plan that he would get to a place where they spoke English and they would be impressed that he could already speak it. 'Good morning,' he would say, as he left to head out into the city. 'Good evening,' he would say when we came back together that night.

Everyone was shuffling, elbowing, trying to gain enough room to sit comfortably. It made me think of Reza, of how he'd saved us that night in the underground barn. He wasn't here to lift us out of the cells and lead us through the snow this time. We had all walked down out of the mountains, sheltering in fields in the day and walking at the side of the road at night. At the bottom of the mountain, trucks came and we were separated as he was shoved into a different truck, and I never saw or heard anything from Reza or any of the people again. I wondered if they had been caught and sent back across the border.

As those in the cell slept, the air full of the smell of their breath and bodies, I watched the men in uniform outside the cell, slumped in their metal chairs, trying to get comfortable by leaning against the walls, their machine guns hanging around their shoulders. The one who had caught me checked on us from time to time before slumping back in his chair. I noticed how vulnerable he looked as he slept. I almost felt sorry for him. *Does he miss his family? Would he behave so viciously towards us if he had a choice?* I wondered. He was like any one of us. A human being – except that we were behind those thick and dusted bars, and he was outside of them. Did that mean that he was free, and we were not? Who would choose to do this to people if they had a choice? Which young child dreams of this as their future? He was just like us: tired, exhausted and snoring in a dirty underground cell – away from his family and alone.

In the morning I was awoken by violent shouting as a new group of armed soldiers marched across the dark hallway shouting and striking everyone with their batons at random, whoever they would reach, until everyone was on their feet trying to shelter behind each other. The officer in front looked at every person sharply while rubbing his fingers against one another, signalling money counting. 'Take out your money and pay for your tickets back home,' they would say. As everyone handed over whatever money they had on them, an older man mumbled from the back: 'Don't give them your money. They will buy tickets with our cash to deport us all back. I'm telling you, just don't give them your money,' the man kept mumbling from the back. The officers continued barking, shouting, and hitting everyone up and down the aisle, demanding more money.

After some fifteen minutes of threats and interrogation, the officers left. Everyone was handcuffed and led onto a large coach. It started moving as soon as it was full. A small amount of fresh air mixed with rainwater blowing in through small holes in the sides of the coach felt strangely hopeful.

The coach continued driving through the bustling city for about forty-five minutes before stopping outside a modern-looking building with automatic double doors and an armed officer sitting in a little station on the side of the road. After the coach was parked, we were ordered to get off and were guided into a large, clean empty room in the corner of the enormous office building – one of the officers stood at the door and watched us as we went past. The barrel of his machine gun hung down at his side. We waited there for hours, until late in the afternoon when a fresh-looking, middle-aged man, dressed in a dark blue suit with a clean blue folder in his hands, appeared at the door of the hallway.

The man's appearance commanded an unshakable level of respect and fear among the guards as they all bowed to him. I was amazed at how this one unarmed man in a clean suit could exert so much power over half a dozen armed soldiers with machine guns. Everyone in the room sat up and our eyes and ears remained fixed to his mouth, waiting for the verdict that would determine our fate. A number of stress wrinkles were carved into the outer corners of his eyes, and his expression seemed to signal some deep-seated tension, perhaps an internal conflict of some sort.

'We-we have decided to-to-to . . .' the man paused, clearing his throat, wetting his dry lips while looking down at the open blue folder before him. I could see he was not reading anything. He was just looking down on the files before him, blank. Perhaps to delay the decision. The pause, only a few seconds, seemed endless. I could feel the heat and sweat on my forehead.

'We have not made this decision lightly, but we have decided not to deport you back to . . . where you are from . . . because we know it is not safe to return at the moment. But on this occasion only . . .' he emphasised. The man's sentence was not completed, yet every single one of the ninety or so people in that room jumped up in celebration as if this man had just promised them the world. Tired, unwashed faces, despairing eyes and dry lips were brightened with smiles and cheers. The silence had turned into joyful prayer, laughter and celebration and a wave of relief shot through me. The room was so abuzz with energy that many didn't hear the man clear his throat and continue to complete his unfinished statement. 'But . . .' the man said, 'you must leave our country yourself – voluntarily.' The man's final words were like a needle in a balloon in the air, rapidly deflating the excitement and hope in the room. 'I am repeating this. You must leave this country yourselves – now.' His forefinger was pointing to the carpeted floor before him. 'Wherever you go, it is up to you. But if you are found in this country again by our officers, I'll have no choice but to deport you back to wherever you came from.' His stern eyes stared, waiting for a response, a confirmation.

Dozens of puffy, watery eyes and tilted heads nodded reluctantly to the man's statement. The man spoke again, his voice laced with frustration. 'Do you agree with me, or do you want me to deport you today?'

'Yes, we agree with you, sir.' Most of us nodded, however unwillingly. But our responses were not acceptable for this powerful official. He wanted us to commit unconditionally to his demands in that moment. No questions. The man repeated for the third time, demanding that we should accept the condition of our release and that we should promise to leave his country immediately. 'This is the last time that I'm going to say this.' Again, we replied, 'Yes, sir.'

The crowd were louder this time, everyone speaking as one in order to satisfy the official, however painful it was. 'Good, now, off you go,' he ordered, gesturing to his officers, who began to move towards us as he left the room, shaking his head.

5

Unknown

'Did you hear that?' Anwar whispered. We were crouched down at the mouth of a railway tunnel trying to hear anything over the sound of our breath, both of us panting like tired dogs. I tried to answer him, but my mouth was so dry I could hardly make a noise.

'Hear what?' I strained my ears, but I couldn't hear anything. It could have been others from the group, or it could be the men from the ambush, come to round the last of us up, to make sure there was no one left who had seen them.

The side of the railway track was slippery, and we were both holding onto thorn bushes to stop us sliding down into the deep gorge. It was our seventh day of hiding during the day and moving at night. We had made it past sniffer dogs and guards wearing night-vision goggles, running as fast as we could, expecting to hear the sound of bullets at any moment. There were just two of us left from our group of Hazara boys, and we had decided to try and get out of Turkey in the same direction, wanting to stick together. We knew which way we were heading, so during the day we hid in the woods, filling our water bottles from streams and eating the tinned food in our backpacks that we'd brought from Istanbul. At night we followed the railway. We listened for the sound of trains, or men with dogs. Several times we had heard something moving in the woods alongside us, keeping pace with us but we just kept jogging. We had heard howls in the distance but we weren't sure if they were wolves or wild dogs.

Anwar put his ear to the railway line, listening for the sound of a train. I stared into the black hole. We had been through two already. What if there were a hundred tunnels? Two desperate runs, as fast as possible, straining to hear the rails humming. We had no idea if there was enough room for a person to fit alongside the track. We had both heard the story of the boy crushed to pieces by a high-speed train inside a tunnel, the train crushing his head and skull in a fraction of a second. The vision flashed across my mind repeatedly. *Where does it hit first? How fast does it happen? Do you feel anything?*

Both times we had been through tunnels before, we had burst out the other end, gasping, our hearts hammering in our chests, laughing with relief.

In the distance, I thought I could hear a stream bubbling. I thought of the times I had sat by the stream near our house but immediately forced myself to think of something else. I did not want to go where that thinking went. I took off my backpack, lay on my back and looked up at the sky. There were so many stars above us, drifting peacefully. It was good to be back out in the clean air after months in the noise and stink of Istanbul. I hoped that the wilderness would mean we were much less likely to meet people.

'I thought I heard the howling again,' Anwar whispered. I ignored him. He turned back, walking silently on the narrow railway, a few metres ahead of me.

'Let's go,' Anwar hissed. He began whispering prayers under his breath as he always did. I stumbled to my feet, pulling my backpack on and started to follow him into the darkness of the tunnel. We ran steadily and I tried to follow the tapping of his feet ahead of me, but they were getting gradually further away. I stopped for a moment to listen but all I could hear was the sound of my own heartbeat and breath. I started sprinting, but immediately slipped on the rail and my backpack got caught on something on the track. For a moment I was trapped, facing upwards. I imagined the train ploughing over me, dragging me underneath. I wriggled violently and was able to get to my feet. But suddenly I wasn't sure if I was facing the same way. I was in the middle of the rails. I turned in both directions. The same unending black. I wanted to call out to Anwar but I imagined my voice echoing out the other end of the tunnel, alerting guards. I could not believe he had just left me. But I knew I would do the same. Perhaps he thought I had been caught, that there were guards in the darkness. I picked a direction and started running, slipping and tripping now, not sure if I was moving forwards or back where we'd come, only caring that I got out of the tunnel. *I had run for much longer now than when I started – surely I was going the right way? But how long was this tunnel? Perhaps this tunnel was miles long, through an entire mountain.* I thought I felt the rail begin to vibrate but I did not want to waste time stopping to check. I just pushed forward even faster. I burst out into the night and just to the side of the track I saw Anwar on his knees, still panting. I was about to laugh with him, when less than fifty metres away there was suddenly a bright light. A train had come round a steep corner out of the woods, shrieking. Suddenly we saw how steep the mountain's sides were and we both crouched in a spot we hoped was far enough away from the track to be safe. The train rushed by us, the roar of metal against metal. It wasn't going to hit us. I tried to stand on my tiptoes, to see in. I could just about see the warm light inside and seats and tables.

'Sit down,' hissed Anwar, pulling me down by my backpack. 'If anyone on that train sees us, they'll call the police.' He pulled us back further from the track and I lost my balance, as I grabbed hold of a branch. The train carried on and on, as if it would last forever, and then it was suddenly gone. The light moved away down the tunnel before it finally disappeared.

Anwar waited, listening for a few moments. 'Let's go, let's go now.'

We both started walking quickly, silently. The track sloped down and eventually I began to clearly hear the sound of running water. We emerged from thick bushes to find a stream beside us. I scrambled down the bank, through trees and knelt in the shallows, drinking the cold water from my hands and splashing it against my face.

'Let's rest for a bit,' said Anwar.

We walked a way along the bank and found a place with flat river stones and dropped our backpacks down. We filled our water bottles and then lay with our heads on our packs resting.

I must have dozed because I was woken by Anwar shaking my shoulder.

'Can you hear that?' His voice was urgent, afraid.

'What?' I asked, dozily, turning away from him.

'Wake up,' said Anwar, pulling things from his backpack. 'Eat something.'

I was still half asleep, the sound of the river taking me to a place of happiness. But he kept poking me, so I rolled upright. He handed me a piece of dry bread and an opened can of fish. He was scooping the same into his mouth.

'Eat, eat, you need to get some energy, you're starving', he said, his mouth full. My stomach groaned and I took the tin. He sat back down facing me, his back to the woods. That's when I heard it.

The sound of something running through the woods just to the side of us. It was as if my whole body was hit by electricity. I jumped to my feet, letting my backpack fall to the floor. Anwar, still chewing loudly, looked up at me with astonishment.

I got my knife out of my pocket. I thought I saw a flash of movement through the trees. I heard something behind me and turned, walking towards the noise to see what it was. Then I heard a growling sound that turned my blood cold. When I turned back towards Anwar, I saw something running towards him. It was just a flash of fur, and I wasn't sure if I saw teeth, but I shouted loudly, waving my arms, sprinting towards him waving the knife in front of me. At any moment, I thought I would see Anwar dragged backwards by the throat or shoulder. I reached him in a few seconds and fell onto him, just in time to watch the animal running away, a tail slipping into the woods and then the sound of howling.

'What the hell was that?!' shouted Anwar, scrambling to his feet. I suddenly felt like I might vomit. My hands were shaking.

I turned back to Anwar to find him urgently pulling things from his backpack.

'I-I can't find my knife,' he said.

'You're not supposed to keep your knife in your bag,' I duly noted. We were told by the smugglers to pack one small automatic pocketknife each.

'I know, but I can't find it now,' he said, his voice shaking.

I didn't know whether to scream, laugh out loud or start crying. For so long there had been so many threats, so much hiding from monsters and soldiers and policeman, and then suddenly there was a real monster and we had beaten it, we had managed to scare it off. I wondered what it must be like to be a creature like that, to be wanted nowhere, for your home to be taken away, to be chased and shot at, while searching for food. I thought of my imagined bargain with the animal. In the distance we heard howling.

We both quickly packed our backpacks and climbed up the bank to the railway as quietly as we could. More howls, this time, though we couldn't tell if the sound was behind or ahead of us. Without speaking, we both broke into a gentle run.

'It was probably a fucking dog,' said Anwar. But he wasn't smiling. In my pocket, I felt the handle of my knife as we continued running into the darkness.

6

Greece

I am lost. Things are appearing and disappearing. *What do I remember?* I am confused. I try to focus hard, to grasp a glimpse of one of the memories that keep flashing in the back of my head before fading away again. I struggle to see the memory in full pictures. Nonetheless, it still seems real, hanging there briefly before dissolving back into nothingness. *Did I see it? Did I experience it? I must have. I did, but it is no longer there, so maybe I did not. Perhaps I was wrong; dreaming, maybe.* I pause for a moment, thinking hard. There is something sensitive on the back of my head, something physical, a burning pain, an injury of some sort. I could be wrong though. Nothing seems real, anyway. So, I stop. *It must be real because I can feel it, feel the pain. Therefore I must exist. I must still be alive. Otherwise, how could it be possible to feel pain if I am dead?*

It is all happening at once – a crowd shouting Allah Akbar. With the muzzled dogs, they force us to sleep in a field of landmines. We must keep still, or we will roll onto the landmines.

There are other people around me – Anwar, Reza, my sister, but they have the faces of the man buried outside the mosque. I am being eaten by the insects that fed on the flesh of the bodies left in a pile. They think I am dead. Perhaps I am.

I can feel my heart pumping, faster and faster, creating a tingling wet feeling underneath the thin hair on my skin, sweat bubbling through each little hair all over my body, drowning me.

Whatever this is, it must be good, because I cannot remember anything. My mind says there is no need to worry. There is something I have to do but my mind keeps telling me it is still all far away. I remember more and more things as I continue to drown in sweat, shivering, then burning. The dark images begin to gain some colour, pale light colours – a life of some sort. I remember soldiers, lots of soldiers, dark images in the corner of an empty port on an island in the middle of the night, staring at me with their sharp eyes, preparing to attack, ambush. I run, run fast. One of them is chasing me. I run faster, so does he. I can hear his breathing, his mouth wide open, panting like a dog right behind my shoulder, growling, attacking. Those flashes fade away too. I feel better, relieved, at least for the moment.

I become aware of people around me.

I sit up to the familiar sight of exhausted men and boys. I do not know how long I have been asleep, or if it has even been sleep at all. I hear the sound of someone marching, policeman or soldiers blurred into one. I stare at the men and boys standing and crouching, shivering and flinching with the sound of marching in the background. I do not meet anyone's eye. Everyone stares down at the ground or straight ahead. I do not know how long I have been here. Some part of me wonders if I have been here forever, dreaming of snow and wolves and cities. I do not know any of these people. I don't know where Anwar is. He was with me when we first got to the camp. I think. We were both sick. Or was that before, at the end of the valley when the police were suddenly among us, their dogs barking? So much running and walking. He isn't here now. Perhaps he has gone back to the tunnel. Perhaps the wolf found him.

I became aware of a fragile voice from among the crowd, somewhere near the green metallic door of the cell:

'Let's call the UN,' he mumbles quietly under his nervous breath. A young boy, skinny. Not much older than me. There is the sound of muttering, some people agreeing, others asking what he had said.

Then another voice.

'Who do you think you are that you think the Uwen, Uwane, whatever that thing is called, will come and help you?' his grin on his long, bony face twisted in disapproval. I couldn't figure out whether his reaction was based on knowing what the boy was talking about or from jealousy because he didn't.

But there is silence, as if a glimpse of hope fades away again. The young boy is weak, he has the sunken cheeks of the starving.

'My name is Nemat. The UN helps people like us.' And he added, 'I have the number, the UN number, but my English is not good to be able to call them.'

'What? What is that thing, binglish, you say?' an old man whispered authoritatively through his *naswar* stained front teeth, causing some of the younger men to suppress smiles, '*Bachem*, my sons, if any of you know how to speak that tongue – binglish, minglish – whatever that is, we should try to call. Who knows? God is kind. There might be someone out there who might be willing to help us,' the old man mutters again, running his fingers through his beard with his wrinkled hand, revealing the remainder of his blackened broken teeth.

'That's right. In Europe, people have respect for human rights, you know,' says Nemat.

I know what many of the separate words mean but he is using them as if they are joined together and have a special meaning.

The old man, who had said his name was Abbas, was looking away, agitated, brushing his long bony fingers over his skinny jaw. I did not know who was right, but I liked the idea of it and somehow felt a tiny glimpse of hope somewhere in the corner of my heart. There had been so much talk of monsters but this was talk of help. Of some sort of group that could help us from another place. I could see the same contemplation on others' faces.

I still only knew a few English words, most of them from Kazim's dictionary, but any time I heard smugglers or boys in the camp speaking English, I tried to learn more.

'I, I can speak a little,' I found myself mumbling when everyone else remained silent, heads down, looking at their hands before them.

'Anyone else?' the old man asked after glancing at me dismissively.

'I can also try,' Nemat, who came up with the idea in the first place, spoke up, volunteering to go out and make the call.

After some negotiation with the guards, Nemat was escorted out of the cell by two armed guards as the rest of us waited anxiously, hoping that he would be able to communicate with this thing called the UN and that the UN would come and help us. Around thirty minutes later, the guards arrived, shouting and kicking the blue metallic cell doors with their boots, demanding that we get out and leave immediately.

We knew if we left the cells and went wherever they were taking us, we would never have a chance to reach out to the UN, so we all decided to resist by stopping the guards from opening the cell doors until Nemat's return. The old man Abbas volunteered to mobilise everyone inside the cell. He seemed to feel proud of taking charge. And I volunteered to communicate with others in half a dozen compartments, situated in tightly packed rows in the dark, damp basement. Through the tiny holes in the cell door, I communicated to the people in other rooms that Nemat has gone to call the UN, who might come and help us, and until then we must stay in our cells and resist evacuation. No one knew what this last bit meant, but they all liked the idea of receiving help, whoever from, and so they agreed to not leave until Nemat returned.

It was Abbas's idea that during our resistance, we should also shout out 'UN, UN, UN', in a united voice from all cells in the underground. At first, the guards appeared, looking lost and confused. They grew suspicious and frustrated at the energy levels building up inside the cells and quickly turned violent, barking more loudly and harshly to distract our communication. Minutes later, a new group of armed officers marched into the basement, their heads protected by thick helmets, as they carried powerful shields and were accompanied by trained military dogs, barking loudly like their officers. They all started attacking the metallic doors. Their voices echoed and reverberated across the suffocating concrete underground cells in waves, meeting the desperate sounds of dozens of displaced boys and men struggling to keep the metallic doors shut while chanting the words: UN, UN, UN.

More officers arrived and the morale inside the cells rapidly declined. Men were shaking and shivering, their faces turned pale, eyes flooded with tears. Abbas sat in silence in the corner of the cell like a child, his lips moving in prayer. The barking, kicking, striking and pushing at the doors continued. Soon after, yet more brutal officers arrived, immediately attacking the nearest cell to the entrance with a huge battering ram, breaking the metallic door and attacking everyone with their batons, mercilessly. The second cell in the same row near the exit resisted, briefly, requiring the attackers to kick in the door. The remaining cells voluntarily opened their doors, each person running outside as fast as they could while the officers hit out wildly at them as they passed, knocking their heads against the corridor walls. Within minutes, all the cells except ours had evacuated.

Through the tiny hole in the middle of the metallic door, I came face to face with a huge man. His dark brown eyes were buried behind his navy blue protective helmet, and he was holding a huge battering ram. He crashed it hard against our door, once, twice, three times. On the third strike the door smashed back against me, throwing me backwards. The door opened. The soldiers ran in, hitting and kicking left and right. We tried to hold onto each other, by the arms, the legs or whatever clothes we could grab. They pounded their sticks against our hands, trying to make us let go. We continued to chant, 'UN, UN, UN.' Then I heard Abbas say, 'Let's go, they are killing us.' He was dragged out by the legs. The huge guard had a dog and was directing it to grab hold of us, and I think I felt its teeth in my leg.

I was dragged backwards along the floor, as soldiers struck me with their boots, their fists and with sticks. It became so there were not individual pains but a fire throughout all of my organs, my ribs and my back. I felt myself being lifted by many hands, as something cracked against the side of my head, the world darkening as I felt myself falling down, half unconscious, as I hit the dirty tiles of the corridor. Then I was dragged, face down, along the corridor, groaning with pain. The noise, the shouting, was echoing off the walls. The ripe smell of unwashed armpits and bad breath brought me back around. Someone was shaking me and I felt a fierce pain from where I had been struck. I opened my eyes. All I saw were dark blue helmets and fierce eyes from behind thick protective glass shields above my face, circling – all looking down at me. Their lips moved in anger, shouting, but I couldn't hear anything. I was lifted underneath the armpits to my feet.

I saw a miracle, a small white plastic cup of water, being handed from soldier to soldier towards me. There is never enough water. My throat has been dry for so long. I imagined how it would feel to drink it. But by the time it reached me, I had already made up my mind. At first, I ignored it but the hands holding me shook me in case I hadn't seen it. The soldier held it out towards me – I reached up and pushed it out of his hands, watched the cup hit the dirty tiles, splashing his military boots.

He shrugged and I was dragged off towards the bus. As I limped towards the back of the bus, I saw Nemat, head down, avoiding eye contact. I looked at him but said nothing. Perhaps Abbas had been right. What Nemat had spoken of was not for us.

Everyone sat in silence, waiting for the bus to pull away. The only sound was the rhythmic tapping of blood as it hit the floor. I tried to drag myself towards the back of the bus where everyone else was, but a pair of powerful hands pulled me back and threw me into a tiny cage just behind the front passenger seat. The engine of the bus revved and we started moving. I thought about the soldier's brutality inside the cell and became angry and started kicking the cage and shouting.

'Shut up!' screamed the officer, banging the cage.

I was in so much pain. What else was there to be scared of? I kept screaming and banging. After some time, when they stopped threatening, I slowly became quiet. I was tired, thirsty, and aching all over. I must've fallen asleep at some point. I dreamed of my mother whispering in the darkness.

ACROSS MOUNTAINS, LAND AND SEA

I cannot remember the details, but I know I was with her back home. Back when I had my childhood and when survival wasn't the sole thing I fought for. When I woke, the bus was still moving, and everyone was as quiet as the dead, their heads tilted sideways, some snoring. Since I had left home, a song had stuck in my mind. I suddenly started singing out loud in the bus:

My dear mother,
You are my beautiful paradise, my soulmate
You are my everything in this world.
I remember your advice, your guidance
To stand up to injustices
And to never give up.

7

The Mediterranean Sea

'We're sinking!' shouted Belal.

I shook myself awake, though I did not know how long I had been asleep. My ribs still ached from the extra hard kick from the police officer the week before, when we had tried to cross by land. We had later been told about men who knew a way by sea.

'What?' I shouted back.

'The dinghy is sinking,' he moaned again.

He was right. We were too low in the water, waves splashing in over the side. The sky and the water were dark now and it was raining hard, not the drizzle we had when we'd set off from shore.

'Where's the pump?' I asked.

'I think it already drowned,' he mumbled.

'We're too low in the water.'

'Please, God . . . please, please save us. I don't want to die. I want to see my mother again,' Belal repeated frantically.

'Nemat, Nemat!' I shouted but there was no answer. No movement or a sign of life.

'He–he is not conscious,' Belal mumbled from the back.

When we had first set off, I had felt hopeful. The sea had been calmer and I had dared to dream that this time we would be lucky. A guide brought the boat and the pump to us and pointed in the direction of some streetlights on the other side of the sea: 'Someone will meet you over there.' He told us to jump in and start rowing. Then began the same game of waiting for someone else to jump into the dinghy first. I remembered how Reza took the lead crossing over the minefield at the previous border. So, when no one else wanted to sit at the front, I volunteered and sat at the front and Belal and Nemat jumped in after me. The three of us started steering the small dinghy into the pitch-black ocean.

I searched all around me in the dinghy with my left hand while holding both oars with my right. With the tip of my fingers, I noticed that the ridged curves, which were meant to be full of air and tight, were loose and wrinkled.

'Nemat!' I shouted again.

I heard a groan. *Thank God, he is still alive,* I thought.

'Worrrrq-worrq . . .' He sounded as if he was throwing up.

'His seasickness has become so bad, but there's nothing in his stomach to throw up, I think,' Belal mumbled.

I pushed past Belal as he tried to stop Nemat from falling out of the dinghy and began searching for the pump. I knew we had to get more air into the dinghy. I saw Nemat's backpack floating around in the water in the bottom of the boat and reached into the side pocket and my my fingertips hit the plastic of the pump.

'I've found it!' I called, my voice cracking.

'I told you that God will respond to our prayers, yes I told you,' Belal exclaimed.

'I need to keep rowing. Can you pump it on your own?' I asked, knowing that there were not any other options, anyway.

'Yes, I can, with God's power. Yes, I can,' he said.

I heard the rasp of pumping and soon the dinghy began to move beneath me, gradually rising up. With the oars,

I tried to keep the boat facing the waves like the smugglers told us.

'Belal, try to get as much water out as you can,' I said.

With more air in it, it was as if the dinghy had come back to life.

'It's pumped up now. I did it, thank God we are alive!' Belal exclaimed.

'Yes,' I replied, nodding my head in the dark.

'Yes, I told you that God is kind. We will reach dry land, somewhere, *inshallah*,' Nemat sobbed.

'We will have to keep pumping,' I said. 'And anyone not pumping or rowing will have to try and get the water out of the dinghy.'

My heart beating fast, I tried to row as the smugglers had told us, my mind a blank. My mouth was dry from the salt water. Every time a wave hit the dinghy from the side, it felt as if it was going to turn over. None of us could swim and though we had life jackets, they were from the same place as the dinghy and I did not feel confident they would stay pumped up. These were children's things, not meant for the sea. I felt a movement behind me as the weight shifted in the boat and then Nemat was behind me.

'Erm . . .' he squeaked reluctantly, clearing his dry throat. I was glad to hear him, that he was still alive, still breathing. 'What's the point? Not even a miracle can rescue us from this. We're all going to drown soon, anyway.'

I was about to say something but managed to stop, as the word was almost out of my mouth. Belal, who was a little emboldened by his heroic bravery of single-handedly pumping the deflating dinghy on the peak of the waves, burst out in anger:

'You can die if you want, coward. But I am hopeful that God will help us survive.' I heard him murmuring swear words.

ACROSS MOUNTAINS, LAND AND SEA

There was a long moment of silence while everything seemed calm as the boat moved along the surface of the sea.

I lost all track of time as I concentrated on keeping the dinghy facing the waves and I heard the sound of pumping. We had long ago given up the idea of steering in any direction, and I couldn't have seen which way to go, even if we knew. The guide had just pointed at the lights and said someone would meet us there. But having been carried away on the wings of sea storms for hours, we could've been deep into international waters by now.

Sometimes the wind would whip up and the waves would be like steep hills, as the dinghy climbed up one side and slid down the other. I remembered the first time I had seen the sea in Turkey. I had never seen so much water, shining as far as the horizon. But I was afraid of the water – I could not swim. I had not even gone into the rivers and streams growing up, as I was scared. The thought of so much endless dark water was terrifying.

I could hear Belal pleading: 'I don't want to die. I want to see my mother again. Please God, help me this time and this time only . . .' Belal had been repeating these lines over and over for several hours until I could no longer hear him as he lost his voice. Nemat, on the other hand, had given up hope hours ago – not just in life but also in God and his ability or intention to help us any more. He did not even bother begging or pleading for help. Perhaps he had lost trust in God altogether long ago. At one point, when the wind and waves were at their fiercest, he whispered behind my ears, 'Let's just drown now. Let's stop suffering.' But when I didn't reply he slumped backwards.

The waves rose either side and lightning illuminated the waves all around us. My eyes were burning from the salt water. I could hardly keep them open. I found myself imagining telling this story and I realised I was telling it to my mother; how hard I had worked to keep the boat facing against the waves.

I would imagine her holding me tight in her arms, kissing me on the cheeks, saying *well done my son, my brave son*. I imagined telling her that Belal was the real hero for keeping the boat pumped up.

At some point, I remembered about the packets of biscuits and bottles of Coca-Cola we had in our bags. I balanced myself carefully on the slick skin of the weakened dinghy and grabbed the bottles of Coca-Cola from my bag. Then, I rummaged in the pocket of my bag and right at the bottom, I found the biscuits mashed up with salty seawater. I gently removed a handful and asked the boys if they wanted some. Belal quickly responded, 'No, I'm not hungry.' He sounded exhausted. He had been pumping for hours.

Nemat did not respond for some time. Then he moved a little, repositioning himself on the flimsy dinghy, causing it to shift before he cleared his throat: 'We are all going to drown at any moment, but there you are having your Coca-Cola and biscuits. Unbelievable!' He stretched out the Coca-Cola part and sighed. I shovelled another handful of biscuit and seawater paste into my mouth, along with most of the bottle of coke. 'Better to die with a full stomach than an empty one, Nemat,' I said before letting out an exaggeratedly loud burp. At some point that night, I saw what I thought were streetlights shining in the distance, and I would immediately try and row towards them, but it was no good. The dinghy was being pulled wherever the sea wanted it.

The others were too sick and dizzy to say or do anything at this point. We had been at sea for almost twenty hours now. Nemat was struggling to hold onto the dinghy or keep breathing, even. Occasionally, I would hear Nemat whispering, praying every time the dinghy was hit by a wave.

'There, there! Look! Look! We're approaching an island, a beautiful city,' I shrieked in confusion, rowing again with full energy in the direction of the lights. I immediately lifted up my chin, shaking my head side to side, clearing my lightning-stricken eyes with my salted wet fingers several times back and forth as I looked again, staring in absolute disbelief. It was right there. Right there in front of us, it must be less than a mile away, straight ahead. This time, much bigger and brighter. The lights getting closer and closer every minute. It was not a hallucination or a dream. It was real. I could see the big bright lights arranged neatly in horizontal rows stretching off into the darkness. The waves around it dancing purple and blue, the white of the wave tips illuminated brightly.

There was hope again. It was difficult to estimate the speed of the dinghy, but I felt it was getting closer to the lights, fast. At times, I was amazed at the sudden injection of powerful energy into my arms that was able to paddle the dinghy this fast towards the lights. *Could it be that that miracle Belal had been praying for throughout the night was finally being delivered?*

I was paddling like crazy, the breath rasping in my chest. As we got closer and closer to the lights, the storm waves seemed to be getting even more violent. The dinghy was once again struggling to stay afloat.

'That—that is not an island. It's a shee–ship. A maaaaa–ssive ship!' Belal shouted from the back. He was right. It was not an island or a city. It was a cruise ship.

We were each supposed to have a torch attached to a string hanging down around our neck to be used for calling for help or warning off any oncoming ships.

'Torch, torch, flash, flash!' I started yelling. I could hear Belal sobbing and praying again, while relentlessly searching for the torch inside his bag. Waves were coming back from the ship, threatening to topple us over.

'Nemat! Nemat! Torch! Torch! Do you have your torch?' I yelled. But there was no answer. I held my oars and bag with my left hand, searching the pockets of my bag with my right hand and still no trace of the bloody torch.

I could hear Belal still searching, praying, and crying for help behind me. One moment he would burst into tears, crying out, 'Please God, help us this time and this time only . . .' Another moment he would cry out, 'Heeelp, Heeelp,' like the desperate sound of a dying goat. The ship continued heading straight towards us. It wouldn't even notice as it smashed straight through us.

After what felt like hours desperately searching, my frozen fingers finally found the torch inside my life jacket. But even when I flashed the light at the ship, nothing happened.

'Flash, flash. For fuck sake, flash the torch!' Nemat barked, unexpectedly, right behind me, which surprised me as I had thought he was no longer interested in life, and wanted us drowned as soon as possible. I kept flashing, but the ship would not respond. It was right there, about one hundred metres away, heading right for us.

We were close enough that the light from our torch was illuminating the white surface of the ship.

'Help, help!' we shouted, as the brightly coloured ship came so close it towered above us. I closed my eyes waiting for impact, but it passed the side of us, only metres away. We waved in the dark, shouting 'Help, help! Heeelp, Heeelp, please help!', hoping that someone would hear us and come to our rescue. But no one did. The ship passed to the side of us, only metres away. It made me think of the train going into the tunnel, of the passengers safe and comfortable in the warm light, while we were outside in the darkness. I thought there was no way they could miss our lights. But they didn't stop.

The dinghy rocked wildly in the wash from the passing ship. Nemat and Belal retreated into silence. They said nothing, did nothing. I was exhausted. Perhaps Nemat was right. Perhaps we should have just given up. What was the point of all this effort only to fail at the end?

Even if we somehow survived this storm and reached dry land somewhere, then what? There would be no hope awaiting us. The only people waiting would be men with guns and dogs, soldiers or police. There would just be a cell, then on to someone else's country. At least here we could make the choice. To stop rowing, to let the sea carry us down.

I stopped rowing, letting the boat rise and fall on the waves. I let my arms and shoulders relax, suddenly aware of how long I had been tensing them.

Death no longer felt as horrifying as it had done. I felt lighter and relaxed. There was no need to continue fighting. Striving. Surviving. No wonder Nemat had been so calm and relaxed all this time amid all this chaos in the storm, while Belal and I panicked. He had already accepted it.

I imagined how it might happen . . . The waves crashing over the dinghy for the final time, tipping it one way, then the other before we fell into the sea. Nemat goes down first, drowning silently without complaining; gracefully even. Belal shouting before his head gets covered by water. He surfaces a few more times to breathe once more before going down forever. Forever. Both gone.

I would float for a while, but then a shark would rise up through the water. Perhaps he would bite me in half, leaving me floating on the surface, my legs gone. Or perhaps it would be so big it would eat me whole.

As I sat thinking about my new journey into the next world to find peace, an image of my mother flashed before my eyes, her light brown eyes wet with tears. The wrinkles around her eyes, her dark blue headscarf.

I wanted to tell her how sorry I was for not being able to continue fighting. I was ashamed that I had not been able to keep going. I was not as strong as her. She had pretty much raised us alone, in the storms of the fighting, the drought and the blockade. She suffered but she never gave up. She would always say: '*Everything will pass on if you do not give up. Never stop fighting, no matter how difficult it may be. God is kind, and justice will be restored one day.*'

And suddenly I knew that I would not give up. In the distance I could see the sky lightening, thick layers of cloud being chased away by a strong wind. It brought hope but it also buffeted our little dinghy even more and it was even worse now. At this final moment, when I knew I did not want to give up, I battled again to stop the dinghy being tossed upside down.

When the morning light came, it showed the full scale of the storm. Huge green waves, tipped with white, like wings, lifting us high into the air before crashing us down again.

Belal began to moan again. 'Oh God, please help . . .' Like the dinghy, his screaming voice was disappearing under the splashing waves. I heard Nemat coughing right behind my ears. Part of me had wondered if we would find he had thrown himself into the water overnight.

I saw a monstrous wave coming towards us and reached for my oars but could only find one. Rowing with one, I called back.

ACROSS MOUNTAINS, LAND AND SEA

'Get the other oars! We have to keep rowing!' I barked.

'My rowing stick fell into the sea during the night,' Belal mumbled.

'Nemat, what about you?' I asked.

'I threw everything into the sea,' he murmured through his nose.

'What? What do you mean? Why??'

'My rowing stick, backpack, lifejacket, the pump. All gone,' Nemat said indifferently. 'I told you – not even a miracle can rescue us, so why the hell are we still trying? You didn't want to die, so go ahead and row,' he barked back as if it was my fault for not letting us drown.

Somehow with only one set of oars, and without pumping, we still did not sink. Though we continued to sink deeper and deeper into the water.

Looking over my shoulder, I could see Nemat lying at the edge of the dinghy. Belal was silent, his fingers white where he was holding on so tightly. Both of them were soaked with water, shivering and pale. My whole body felt numb, but I kept moving the oar. Even if just to try to keep warm. I just didn't want to give up. We lay in silence.

It must have been sometime later in the afternoon, just before sunset, when the dinghy began gaining speed. It was moving faster and faster, even without paddling. In the distance I saw something grey and sat up. Another ship? But it was land. Unbelievably, it was land.

'Land!' I shouted, expecting to get a happy response but I heard nothing, not even them moving to look. So I shouted again, louder this time, but still heard nothing. I kept rowing while looking ahead. It was real. It really was a dry piece of land, an island of some sort. Not like last time – I could really see it. I couldn't keep the excitement down. I wanted Nemat and Belal to see what I saw, to understand there was hope. I shouted again, 'I swear to God, that is dry land.' Still no response, so I stopped shouting.

As we got closer, I could see more and more. There were paved roads and lamp posts along the narrow path, some trees, and a few houses. The waves were suddenly violent. I tried to row us away from the rocks, towards the gentler seafront but it was no good.

I watched a red van appear then disappear on the road along the seafront. I could only see it at the top of each wave and I shouted and waved my hands. 'Help! Help!'

When we hit the rocks, there was a huge crunching feeling. I tried to jump off but my legs wouldn't work from kneeling in the cold water for so long. I pulled myself off the dinghy and tumbled into the cold black of the water, the lifejacket dragging me back up. I tried to grab hold of the dinghy but my hands had nothing to cling onto. I tried to breathe but there was only water, burning my lungs, making me cough and breathe in more water. My clothes were heavy, dragging me down and there was too much water. I turned frantically but couldn't see anything, not the dinghy, not Nemat or Belal, just the waves pulling me down into the stomach of the sea.

8

Greece

It was early in the morning. Before dawn. I tried to squeeze myself up into the underside of the truck, in among the wires and metal. There I would be safe from the freezing wind coming off the sea and the eyes of the border guards.

'The further underneath the truck you are, the more chance of getting past the dogs and electronic sensors at the check-points,' the long-nosed, skinny-faced smuggler had whispered to me. 'Remember to hold your breath and cover your nose with your hand so the dogs don't smell your breath.' I watched his shadow following him among the long lines of parked trucks on the port, as he disappeared. I never saw him again.

I curved my body up into the metal of the truck, uncomfortable, anxiously waiting for the morning to arrive. I did not know which parts of the truck would move, whether I would be dragged up into the truck and pulled apart. There had been a story just days before of a skinny fifteen-year-old boy who had been found squashed to pieces under a heavily loaded truck. With the truck above me, I couldn't help imagining what it would be like to be crushed by its great weight, dragged along for miles, until you were blood on the cement.

The smuggler had said that this truck would go on the right sort of ship. Of course, there were no guarantees this was true, that the ship would turn up, and that this truck would enter it. Perhaps it would drive back into the country I had just come from. Perhaps it would go on a ferry going back over the sea we had crossed in the dinghy.

My ears remained alert to the faintest sounds around me, even the rustle of the yellow leaves on the concrete floor, but it was the footsteps of a soldier I was listening out for. Every time I slept, I would wake, thinking I had heard their footsteps. As I dozed, I thought of Belal and Nemat. I wondered what had happened to them along the way. Did they get caught up by the police and deported back?

Once we had made it out of the water, we had headed to the woods nearby and remained there until it was dark. When night fell, Belal volunteered to go to a phone box and call the number he had. He came back with some food and tickets, with directions that we should go to the port individually in order to reduce the risk of being caught. He said there would be someone there to meet us at the other end of the journey. When it was time to leave, no one volunteered to go first. So, again, I led the way. I never heard anything from them since.

It was late in the afternoon, just before sunset, when the shadows of the other trucks were still dark on the concrete when I heard a door slam close by. The engine started revving and shaking and there was a loud hissing noise. The metal all around me started to raise up and then lower down until it was only a couple of inches away from my face. There was the smell of diesel fumes and hot grease as the truck began to pull away slowly. Every time the truck hit a bump, or stopped and started, there would be a loud sound of metal on metal and the truck would squeeze together, like a jaw clenching. I began to whisper prayers, and managed not to shout out. Eventually we were in a long queue of trucks and the engine idled. I heard footsteps.

Gradually, we moved forwards in the queue. I could hear the same questions and answers, and see men with torches shining lights under the truck.

Every time the truck moved, my heart rate increased. I worried I would pee. I was trapped in a cacophony of voices, of doors opening and closing, of rattling locks as they checked the back doors of the trucks. I thought of those metal boxes they had moved us in, the same boxes that I had seen at every port, at every lorry park. Perhaps there were people in the truck I was hanging underneath. There were so many stories of people in boxes, baking in the sun, or freezing, or dying of thirst. I had heard that five people had been locked in a truck that stayed parked for five days on a blisteringly hot day and they had all perished. Maybe I was better here . . . We moved forwards and then the engine turned off. The truck shuddered and sunk down as the engine stopped. I pressed myself as tight to the lorry as I could, my face pressed against the warm, hard metal.

I heard someone scrabbling down the side of the truck and pressed myself even further up into the wires and the stink of machinery, until I felt like a part of it. I held my breath and covered my nose and mouth tightly with my hand. I could hear someone poking something sharp against the metal below me and I shivered, willing him to miss me. The sound got louder and louder. It must have been only inches away. I felt the point of the metal hit my leg and bit down on hand. Then it swung up and jabbed against my head, three times in a row. They must realise now. That I was not made of metal. At any moment, I would hear the shouting and be dragged out. I just stayed frozen, my eyes filling with tears as the stick or whatever it was poked and scratched into my head. I was running out of breath, and I thought I might faint.

71

Then all of a sudden, the poking stopped and the footsteps moved away. The engine started and the truck rose, cradling me tight. The wheels started rolling and the truck bumped over a hollow metal platform, up at an angle that made the truck hiss and clang. I couldn't believe I had made it onto the ferry. The truck stopped and the door opened and closed. I heard someone calling out to someone else. The sound of truck after truck moving onto the ferry continued for what seemed like many hours. The smuggler had told me that the ship would travel for approximately forty hours to the next port, where there would be another search. It hardly felt like we were on the sea at all, only a slow, repetitious up and down motion. It was nothing like our dinghy.

For almost two days, I stayed completely still, holding onto the metal of the truck. I shifted position, so that I was further up under the truck, balanced over a thick metal pole. My entire body was numb. I was weak with hunger, and my mouth was dry. I dozed in and out of dreams where I had tasks but could never accomplish them.

I woke up to the sound of voices and engines and after a while, trucks started moving down the ferry ramp and out into sharp sunlight. Then the check commenced for the second time. I squashed my body up and up, trying to get away from the sunlight, whispering prayers. This time the check was over much quicker than expected. The truck was on the road quickly in a long line of other vehicles. I was through another border. As the truck began gaining speed on the motorway, I started to regret switching position the night before. Now I was facing downwards towards the ground, watching the fast-moving road pass beneath me at a deadly pace. I had to grasp hold of the metal to stop from falling. I was growing weak. If I kept my eyes open, my head would spin. But when I closed my eyes, it was worse. My ears were full of the roar of so many trucks and cars all around. It had been four days and nights underneath the truck without food or water and I felt sick, weak and dizzy. It was completely possible that soon I would no longer be able to continue holding on and would fall under the wheels of the trucks. At this point I thought it would have been easier and less painful if the waves had taken me.

The truck drove for hours as the bright sunshine turned pale and colourless, and gradually faded. The lights on either side of the road barely reached underneath the truck, passing rapidly like distant lightning.

We reduced speed at one point and I heard movement further down towards my feet. A boy squeezed down from under the truck and caught my eye, his face covered in dust and grease.

'*Khowa Hafiz.*' Goodbye, he said in Kurdish, as he rushed away from the truck across the road, zigzagging among the vehicles before quickly disappearing. I didn't move and the truck started up again. I concentrated on holding on as the road began to blur, the world shrinking to just my arms and the metal.

I sat, too exhausted to run, as white birds cried above us. The man in the bright yellow vest stood over me.

'Do you speak English?'

I nodded.

'A little.'

Behind him, the sun rose and I squinted up at him. My mouth was dry. I wondered if he would beat me.

'Where are you from?'

He asked again, his voice gentler.

'Where are you from?'

*

I thought of the days that had led here, blurring into one. Of moving, sometimes underneath trucks, sometimes in the back of them. The dull light of motorways. Slipping out at traffic lights in the middle of nowhere, at places where the drivers stopped to sleep. Inside vehicles designed to transport things around the world. To bring boxes full of things that people wanted – food, goods, medicine. Things made in other countries, brought to this one.

And now they had brought me here. The white birds cried above me.

'Where are you from?'

I lay back down and closed my eyes.

Part Two

9

London

The three of them sat in a line opposite me across a heavy wooden table in a room lined with books. The air smelt of hot dust. Two men and a woman. The older of the two men spoke first, smiling.

'No need to be nervous . . .' He checked the paper in front of him. 'Mr Azadi, this is our chance to get to know you, ask you a few questions and for you to ask us anything you'd like to know at this stage.'

I am wearing a suit that does not fit me. I have prepared so much to say, but I suddenly cannot find the words.

'It says here you went to school in Herne Bay. How lovely.'

I nodded.

'Well, why not start there. Why don't you tell us a little about school? What brought you here?'

10

Kent, 2001

'Arman, come on. Wake up, you're going to be late.' Charlotte knocked on the bedroom door until I groaned in reply. I lay there. It felt as if I'd only just got to sleep. All night I had been lost in nightmares, being chased by dogs down long corridors, waking up with the feeling of salt water in my throat. I had nightmares often but they had been especially bad that night. It had been the look of fear on the faces of the adults that had brought the nightmares . . .

We had all been sitting around the television the night before, watching the news. The footage of planes flying into a building. The night staff at the youth hostel were shaking their heads and looking sad and serious. But worst of all was the fear.

I asked if there had been an accident.

A couple of the boys who spoke more English shook their heads. They said it was deliberate. It was an attack. One boy whistled as he said it, as if whoever did it had made a grave mistake. He said, 'The Americans will be angry now, just watch.' The same images, of the bright blue sky, the silver buildings and the plane. The dark smoke.

I could not understand the television. They spoke too fast and I couldn't work out what I was looking at. Some of the boys sat for hours watching it, said it was good for learning English. But I stayed in my room. There were two of us in the bunk bed but beyond nodding when we first saw each other, we didn't speak. When he got up in the morning, I could close the door and stretch out on the bed. There were places for my clothes. Everything was clean.

Television was just one of many things I could not understand. The food, the trays, and the things they gave you to eat with. It took a while to get used to those things. You could tell how long a person had been at the hostel from how quickly they finished their meals.

Even when I could understand, I didn't know what the other young people talked about. There were so many things I didn't know, so I just watched and listened, nodded and smiled.

'Come on, Arman. Hurry up. And don't forget your school uniform.'

I got out of bed and opened the curtains. I observed the still-strange countryside outside, so flat and green. The tree trunks so thick with so many leaves. Charlotte had said that the place we were in was called 'the garden of England'. On some of the rare sunny days, I would sit on the grass just behind the hostel for hours and look out at the trees and the fields that stretched as far as I could see. The endless green. This morning a watery sun was just about making its way through clouds, as it had been for most of the time I'd been here. Summer had passed and I hadn't even noticed. It had been just over two months since I had arrived in Britain.

That first morning, the man in the bright yellow jacket had taken me away from the truck and down to a small hut. He gestured for me to sit down on a white plastic chair next to several other men who were covered in engine oil, saying something about 'a driver'. There were no soldiers but I wondered where they would drive us to. A camp? A prison? Perhaps there would be a man with a folder who would send us on to the next place. I wasn't sure if men would come to check if we had money, to beat us, to bring dogs close to us. The man with the bright yellow jacket came back with a plastic cup of water and gave it to me. I waited until he was gone to drink it.

After a short while, another man came in and beckoned me over to a minibus that drove me to a clean, modern-looking building where more people dressed like us were waiting in lines. When I got to a counter, a tired-looking woman asked me questions in English. I could not understand much but I could tell she was asking where I was from and how old I was, and whether I was with my family. Just as the sun was setting, I was taken to a building full of individual rooms with beds, where there were clothes laid out. I stood in the shower and let the water run over my head, cleaning the dirt and greasy oil from my hair and body. I slept on a bed with white sheets and when I woke up, I couldn't work out where I was. I could hear people moving about around me but there was no shouting or dogs barking.

I went downstairs and ate in the small dining room. Then a woman came and introduced herself as Julie. I didn't really understand what she was saying but she asked me the same questions as before but in slightly different ways. She kept checking my age and where my family was. I told her I didn't know.

Julie took me out of the room and we drove for a couple of hours. Everything was pale and grey-green. As she drove, she sang under her breath to songs.

We arrived outside a low brown building, where a smiling woman with bright eyes and brown hair was holding a folder. She introduced herself as Charlotte and asked me my name.

'Let's get you settled and then it'll be time for dinner. You can meet some of the others. That's where they serve meals.' She gestured into a room with tables.

She took me to a small room with bunk beds.

'Top one's free,' she said, smiling. 'The boy who lived here has just moved on,' she said. *Moved on! Where to?* I wondered.

Out of the window I could see people kicking a football on the grass.

I nodded and smiled at her. I climbed up onto the bunk bed and shut my eyes. A couple of times there were quiet knocks on the door but I ignored them. The next day, I collected a plate of food and ate alone without meeting anyone's eye. I did not have the energy to talk to anyone.

After a couple of days, Charlotte knocked on the door and explained I needed to get dressed and come with her. She was smiling and I followed her down a corridor until she knocked quietly on one of the doors and put her head around the door. She gestured for me to go in and squeezed my shoulder. 'No need to be nervous. Good luck.'

As I entered the room, there were three men in neat dark suits with ties. They were sitting around a table covered in papers and pens and gestured for me to sit down. I could feel the air thickening around me, my chest tightening with every heartbeat. One of the men looked up and nodded at me to sit. He could have been the cousin of the man in Istanbul, the same professionally tired look on his face, the same angle of his neck looking down at the paper in front of him. All that was missing was the thick moustache.

I felt sad that it had been Charlotte that brought me here. Now I know why she had said not to be nervous. She had seemed kind. Sometimes, she would come and find me if I was in the dining room and would try to ask me questions about where I was from, what I liked doing. But I just nodded or shook my head. But now I knew she was on the side of the men with folders. I desperately wanted to pull the door open and run away, back to my room and pull the cover over my head but I was frozen to the spot.

'Please take a seat,' I heard the man muttering softly on the other side of the table, a laptop open in front of him. 'Please take a seat,' said another man with brown eyes sitting on my side of the table in a language that sounded familiar. I had heard different versions of this language somewhere along the way when our truck was first chased and then stopped in deserts in the middle of the night by men with guns demanding money or be shot on the spot.

In front of me there was a white mug, stained brown on the inside, filled with water.

'Do you understand?' I heard the thick-voiced man next to me uttering. I almost jumped up in fright. 'Did you understand what Mr Richard has been explaining?' he said slowly, glancing at the man opposite the table.

'Yea-yes-yes,' I responded abruptly without thinking.

'My name is Mr Kaihani. I will explain what he is saying. Where are you from, what languages do you speak?'

'Afghanistan,' I said. 'I am Hazara and I speak Hazaragi.'

He shook his head. 'They won't have anyone that speaks that here. Do you speak Farsi?'

'A little,' I said.

As soon as the weight of responding to the urgent question was over, my mind began rushing to recall what Mr Richard had just explained, that I had responded yes to.

'Well, at any point during the interview, if you have questions, or if you do not understand, please let us know.' I heard Mr Richard saying something in English before Mr Kaihani turned it into language I was supposed to understand. For me, both languages were foreign but the second one was just a little less so. To begin with, I tried to ask questions to truly understand what Mr Richard was saying but there were many words I did not understand at all, and as I went back and forth with Mr Kaihani, I could feel the other two men getting frustrated – one looked at his watch. If they did not like me, perhaps they would send me to a worse place. I decided to just nod.

Through the corner of my eyes, I would watch Mr Richard typing on his laptop and the man next to him, who introduced himself as a Home Office officer, kept staring at me, his sharp blue eyes fixed on me, mouth closed in a straight line, and both hands placed on top of each other, watching me.

'Do you have questions?' Mr Richard asked after about forty-five minutes' questioning. All I wanted to ask was, *Can I go back to my bed, please?* But I did not say that. 'No,' I responded. It took him another few minutes to explain about these things called the Home Office's procedures, but I couldn't understand much of it, just that they would decide where I would be sent next.

'How long? I asked Mr Kaihani.

He shrugged. 'Sometimes months, sometimes years.'

The interview was over, and I was the first to get out of the little room. On my way down the corridor, I saw Charlotte behind the glass window, sitting inside the hostel's office, looking down at the table in front of her, reading something, perhaps. She immediately rushed out when she saw me outside her office. 'How did it go?'

'OK,' I replied, heading out.

'Would you like some breakfast?' she called after me.

'No, thanks,' I said as I walked away. I went to my room and climbed up onto my bed and pulled the cover over my head and slept.

*

Time passed both quickly and slowly. I hardly got out of bed. I needed all my strength to build the concrete wall that kept the nightmares at bay. Any single crack and the memories would find a way through.

I lay almost lifeless on my clean bunk bed, staring out of my window at the white sky until it darkened and I could sleep. I was taken to see a doctor, who asked me questions. The doctors put needles into me, sometimes taking blood away, sometimes putting things in. I decided that they would not put all this effort in if it was something bad. I had an interview with a woman who asked about my family and I told her everything I could about our village, where it was. There was a place on the form for my address and I couldn't find the words to tell her that an address would not work there.

'Well, we'll do what we can,' she said.

Sometimes a member of staff, Charlotte, would come to check on me, informing me about dinner time or to invite me to join other kids for planned excursions out of the hostel like swimming or playing football, but I did not want to do any of those things. All I wanted was to sleep on my bed without interruption for days and nights on end. At mealtimes, I found an empty table and ate quickly before going back to my room.

One lunchtime she came to find me, accompanied by one of the interpreters, and I could tell she was nervous. She handed me a large envelope.

'This is a letter for you,' she said. I opened it and took out a thick stack of paper with the word Home Office at the top of it. I handed it to Charlotte and she took the top page, her eyes moving over it quickly. She started smiling.

'Congratulations,' she said, her eyes sparkling with excitement.

'What – what is this?' I asked, feeling confused.

'This is your indefinite leave to remain,' she said.

'What–what does that mean?' I asked.

'That means you can stay in this country for as long as you want now.'

I picked up the letter and looked at it but only understood a few of the words. I folded it neatly and put it back in the envelope. My eyes filled with tears and I sat with my head down at the table trying to make them go away. I had not realised, but so much of me had been preparing for the next part: for the train, the lorry or the bus, for the next compound, for running or walking, for sitting on the floor behind a chain-link fence, for not knowing anything other than where I was, would not last forever. Charlotte sat in silence with me and reached out and very briefly squeezed my hand.

'Arman?' said Charlotte, poking her head round the door. I was standing, staring out of the window, wearing my new school uniform.

'Well, look at you, very smart,' she said.

I sat in the minivan, as Bill, a giant, friendly man with a generous belly hanging over his trousers, drove us to the two schools that children from the hostel went to. There were many boys older than me at the hostel who didn't have any-where to go at all.

'Right,' he said. 'That's you.'

I stood watching the van drive away, gripping the piece of paper with grids of numbers and words on it that would tell me where I had to be. There were so many children walking into the building, laughing and shouting and screaming. I thought of the only other classroom I had ever been in; I wondered if the teachers twisted your ears when they were unhappy with you here. I was nervous and afraid but there was also something else. I realised I was excited.

11

First School, Tonbridge

'Where are you from?'

I was surrounded by faces, some smiling, some frowning. The words merged into each other; they were speaking too quickly. A couple of people put their thumbs up at me and smiled, so I did the same. Two boys said something to me but I didn't understand what they meant, so I put my thumbs up and smiled. Everyone went silent. I glanced about me at a lot of unfriendly faces and people shaking their heads but I didn't know what had happened.

That morning I had arrived at the classroom and immediately been surprised that girls and boys were in the same room. Clutching my piece of paper, I had stood at the front of the room, looking at boys and girls sitting next to each other behind rows of white desks. The teacher was a young woman with blue eyes and blonde hair, wearing a pink shirt and long black skirt. She gestured for me to come to her and held out her hand for my letter. The children were talking loudly and laughing. She read the letter and asked me a couple of questions about my name but I couldn't understand them, so I just nodded and smiled.

'Everybody, this is Ama, Aman.' As she stumbled over my name, I heard the sound of suppressed laughter from the back of the room and felt uncomfortable.

She said something to me and gestured towards a desk and I guessed she meant for me to sit there but the only spare seat was next to a girl. I could see that some of the desks did have girls and boys sitting next to each other but I didn't know what the rule was.

I walked slowly towards the empty seat she pointed at, looking behind me at the teacher for confirmation that that was where she really wanted me to sit. I tried to catch the girl's eye, waiting for permission to sit down.

'Hurry up,' said the teacher.

I sat down, feeling as if I had already got things doubly wrong. I had sat down too slowly and now I was sat next to a girl, which felt strange. I could feel the eyes of some of the boys looking at me, whispering behind their arms. One boy called something out that made everyone laugh, but the teacher talked back to him with a sharp voice. The girl next to me nodded at me and said something but I couldn't understand, so I just nodded back.

I could tell that the teacher was trying to control the class but some of the children were ignoring her. She wrote things on the white board and called out questions. Some people put up their hands and she called a name and they answered. But most of the time she was just trying to get the loud children to be quiet. There was no fear in the room and many of the children didn't treat her like an adult but like she was an equal. At one point she made one of the boys leave the room and he made everyone laugh rolling his eyes as he left, dragging his bag over the desks.

Suddenly there was the loud sound of a bell and everyone burst to life, putting things into bags and standing up from their chairs. I followed everyone outside into a yard where some of the children were kicking a football, some were eating on wooden benches. A couple of people asked me things and I just nodded and smiled. I was amazed at how loud and full of energy they all were. They were so confident. I saw a boy spitting on the floor and thought for a moment of Kazim and his dictionary, of how much better prepared he would be. Of how much he would have wanted to be here. But I immediately closed the wall around him. A crowd of children had started to gather.

One of the loud boys from the classroom came over and said something that made his friends laugh. Then he called out to me and I put my thumbs up. And that's when everyone became quiet.

The rest of the day passed in a blur as I walked about the school, showing people my timetable and letter and then being taken into different rooms. There was the same process of laughing and nodding and smiling. Of questions I couldn't understand. Then the bell rang and everyone ran laughing from the building, calling out to each other, pushing and pulling. And it was just me waiting for the minivan to arrive. On the way back, some of the other boys were talking and laughing and some started singing songs but I slept with my face against the window.

When we got back to the hostel, I barely made it upstairs to my room before I lay face down on my bed in my uniform and fell asleep.

I was at dinner with one of the boys I had made friends with called Ehsan when I heard the sound of a familiar voice: Safi, one of the interpreters.

'Lexi wants a quick talk with you,' he said.

I followed Safi down to the office, rubbing my eyes, and found Lexi sitting behind a desk. She spoke to Safi in short sentences and he translated back and forth.

'Have a seat please, Arman.' She licked her lips and cleared her throat. 'We have to ask you something about school today. Do you understand?' I nodded.

'How was school?'

'OK,' I said, not knowing how to say that I had no way of knowing what it was supposed to be like.

'Are you sure?'

Safi nodded encouragingly at me.

'Yes, I think so.'

'We've received a report of an incident. At breaktime.' I just looked at her. 'We need to know what you said to your classmate in the playground.'

'Nothing.'

'Are you sure?'

I nodded.

'So you didn't say anything to anyone about the tragic incident in New York, the planes hitting the towers?' I tried to remember if I had but I was sure I hadn't.

'Listen, *jan kaka*,' Safi said. 'Lexi is saying that they have received a report from the school that you've been telling things to your classmates about yesterday's attack on the twin towers.'

'Haa.' I let out a confused noise through my throat.

'But, but what, what have I said?' I asked. Safi looked at Lexi again and she nodded.

Safi cleared his throat again and said, 'When some boys asked your opinion about the tragic incident in the United States yesterday, you responded with your thumbs up.' He gestured to show me. 'This is saying it was a good thing.'

I thought of the tall boy who had shouted at me, how his friends had laughed.

'This is a very serious issue and I worry that if anything happens to you, we might not be able help you,' Safi translated for Lexi. I just nodded my head.

*

I went back to my room and sat on my bunk. What did she mean by: 'if anything happens to you'? I decided it was just too dangerous not to be able to speak English.

I opened my bag and took the textbook out and opened it on the first page. I only recognised a very few words but I kept going.

12

Foster Family, Whitstable

'I'm Noa, nice to meet you,' said a dark blonde-haired woman, smiling and extending her right hand towards me after gently shaking Julie's hand first. 'How are you, all right?' she said calmly, slightly lowering her posture towards me as I stood on the doorstep. I moved a little uncomfortably, lifting my right arm, reluctantly, not sure how else to react or whether to shake her hand. I still wasn't sure what the rules were about men and women touching. The kids at school didn't seem to have any rules, but they weren't a reliable guide on much.

'Arman is a good boy,' Julie said, with an exaggeratedly bright voice, nodding at me while looking at her hand, so I shook it.

'Come in please, come in,' Noa said, her hand gesturing into the house. Julie walked in first and I followed her through the short corridor into a neat, bright room.

'Please take a seat.' Noa invited Julie to sit on a single cream chair facing the TV, which was switched on, showing people in a studio sitting on sofas. To her side was a wide window onto the quiet street outside. There was a very wide chair the same colour facing a fireplace with what looked like plastic wood in it.

'Feel free to have a seat,' said Noa as she rushed out into the corridor.

'How do you take your tea?' she called in.

'Just milk, no sugar please,' Julie said, as she continued talking.

'How about you, Arman?'

'Milk, and two sugar please,' I said in a low voice. I continued to stare at the TV, not really paying attention to what they were saying but just to look busy.

'Arman is a good boy,' repeated Julie. 'He's doing very well at school,' she added. 'And his English is improving really quickly,' she said before turning to me. 'Isn't it, Arman?'

I pretended I was busy watching the TV and not listening to their conversation. I had learned enough English to get the sense of most things, but my writing was slow. One day a teacher had sent me to the library to read a book and I had gone there for every lesson for weeks, not realising they had just meant for that lesson. I had even sat in a hall as the other students took exams, even though I barely understood the words on the page.

I made a small noise of agreement.

In the last few months, I had made my way through the books they gave me, starting at page one and reading until I got to the end. I had borrowed a dictionary and looked up every single word I did not understand. At first, that was almost every word. But slowly, the list got smaller. When I finished the book, I went back to the beginning and started it again. I wanted to get to a place where I would not have to look up a single word or to ask someone to explain a single idea. And slowly I was beginning to understand the questions in class. I was still frequently puzzled by words and concepts that everyone else seemed to know effortlessly but I no longer spent most of my time nodding and smiling. I had even raised my hand a couple of times to answer questions in class.

At the hostel, I had stopped staying in my room and avoiding eye contact and had even gone on excursions a couple of times. I still felt the wall in my mind, but it felt strong, as if there were no cracks in it. I could go entire days at a time without a flash of something from my past. There were still the nightmares – endlessly running to get somewhere that was too far away, or being in the sinking boat, the water always just about to break over the edges of the dinghy, to drag us down into the darkness. I would wake panting, bitter seawater in my throat. But there were some nights without any dreams at all. Long, cool nights, smooth like unbroken concrete.

I had also made friends with a few of the other boys: Nabi, Ali and Ehsan. Nabi had arrived a few weeks after me and I had noticed him because he was so skinny, his clothes never seemed to fit. His skin was pale and malnourished, his bones seemed to jut out of him. I heard him speaking the same language as me to the interpreters in a familiar accent and was surprised to hear him telling them he was fourteen years old. In spite of his height, he had the body of a child. He would rarely talk to the other boys either. In the early months, I hardly saw him at all as we both stayed in our rooms, but one time I went into the room with the TV and he was there, his head tilted to one side watching a Bollywood film. I watched with him for a few moments.

'I don't really understand it,' I mumbled quietly after a while, feeling a little embarrassed at my English.

'What?' I vaguely heard him muttering underneath his breath, his head still tilted sideways, resting on his right shoulder.

'That,' I said, pointing at the TV. He stayed silent.

'Where are you from?' I asked.

He said the name of the city I had hidden outside in the abandoned mosque. I shivered physically, staring at the multicoloured dancers. Suddenly there were cracks in my wall.

I glanced at him and saw he was watching me.

'I'm not watching this,' he said, before throwing the remote control at me without looking. He closed his eyes and sank back into the worn sofa, hugging his arms to his little body and letting all the air out of him. I put the remote control down and left him, on the broken grey couch. Eyes closed. Motionless. I went upstairs and lay on my bed, breathing and trying to fall asleep.

I had heard that Nabi had been the first to get a school placement, even though he was an unaccompanied children had no previous education or examination results. When school started, I would often find him reading thick textbooks, mostly about science and maths. I wished I could understand those enormous books, like him. We had got into the habit of doing our homework together side by side; sometimes I would ask him for help and sometimes he would help me. Ehsan would try to get us to go outside and play football or play cards, anything other than reading those boring books! We never talked about the past, even though we spoke in Hazaragi to each other sometimes. We both decided we wanted to practise our English. I asked him if he ever got lonely and he told me that his grandfather looked after him.

One day, Nabi gave me his large English dictionary to borrow to look up some words I didn't understand. He let me keep it for months, as I came home from school every day with more words I needed to know the meaning of. Curriculum, mock exams, revision. Results, predicted grades. I felt as if I had barely had time to realise what was happening.

When I had gone to see him to tell him I was going to see a foster family later in the week, he had shrugged.

'Don't forget to give me back my dictionary.'

I listened to Noa and Julie speaking as I stared at the TV screen.

'Here we go.' Noa put the tea on the small table in front of me.

'Thank you,' I mumbled, still looking at the TV screen.

'I'm sure there's a cartoon on somewhere. I'm sure Jared can find some when he gets back.'

As soon as I heard the name 'Jared', I began wondering who he was and if he older or younger. I wondered how he would respond to me. How many other children would there be here? Julie had explained to me on the way there that Noa was someone who looked after children who did not live with their families. Some, like me, because their families were in a different country but some when their family home wasn't the best place for them to live.

As if she read my mind, Noa said, 'Jared's at his after-school football club but should be home soon. Then we've got Ella.'

'Ella?' Noa called out.

'Yaaaaa?' I heard a girl's voice from somewhere in the house.

'Come here and meet Arman,' Noa shouted.

'Okaaaay, comiiiiing.'

Moments later, a lovely little girl appeared in the doorway, looking at me. 'This is Arman, say hi to him,' Noa said.

'Hi Armaaaan,' Ella smiled and waved and I saw her finger-nails were painted purple. I could tell she was desperate to go back to whatever she was doing in the other room.

'You can go now if you like,' Noa said to Ella. 'And then we've got Rajab, who should be on his way back from school.' Julie had already told me about Rajab on the drive over and it was him I was most nervous of.

'He's from your country, not too far away from where you grew up,' she'd said and I'd nodded.

'He's happy to meet you . . . but . . . but . . .' Julie glanced sideways at me to look for my reaction and then looked back at the road. 'He–he's a nice boy, but for some reason he doesn't want you to approach him at school.' She changed gear and slowed down; her eyes were still fixed on the road but was alert to my reaction as I sat next to her silently. 'It's not about you specifically; it's more about anyone from home, I think.'

I'd shrugged but I wondered what it meant.

'And that's all of us, at the moment,' said Noa.

I kept staring at the TV and Julie and Noa continued talking about things I didn't really understand.

After having our tea, Noa invited us to have a look around the house or have 'a little tour', as she called it. There was a clean, neat kitchen facing onto a garden and a dining room with a round table. I could see a computer in the corner of the dining room, just on the right side of the large window overlooking the street in front of the house, which Ella was typing on.

'The kids use this computer for their homework and stuff,' Noa explained to Julie, 'and Arman will be welcome to use it too if he wants, of course,' she added, glancing at me to check my reaction. Inside I was excited but I just nodded in response.

There were four bedrooms upstairs and Noa listed who was in each one before we got to a small room, located right at the top of the house. Noa opened the door and said, 'It's small but it's a lovely little room.' She looked at me with a hint of nervousness. I could see a single bed positioned against the wall, just behind the door, and an old TV, like the one in the hostel, located under the lowered wall in the corner.

'What a lovely view of the garden,' said Julie with an exaggerated tone while looking at me from above her reading glasses. 'So, what do you think?' I nodded solemnly, without saying anything. In fact, I didn't care much about the size of the room or its positioning in the house as long as there was a bed I could sleep in. It was fine with me. I was more worried about how I'd be received by the other children.

'Noa and I were thinking you could try it out for a week. See how it works for everyone and then you could let me know your decision.'

Julie gave me a squeeze on the shoulder and then got in her car, waved and drove away.

'Make yourself at home, Arman. And let me know if you need anything, all right,' Noa said as she walked to the kitchen. I nodded again and sat back on the sofa, still looking at the TV screen. Part of me was happy with what I was seeing: the house was nice and clean, the kitchen was super clean and organised. Noa and Ella seemed nice and friendly, too. But part of me was still unsure and worried about how the rest of the family would receive me. Would Jared like me? And how about this other boy, Rajab?

About half hour later, the door suddenly pushed opened, and I saw a boy entering the house. He started climbing up the stairs immediately. His dark blue backpack hung loose on his right shoulder and his short black hair was spiked up like a boy's at my previous school and one of his eyebrows was cut in the middle asymmetrically. 'Rajab, is that you? Are you back?' I heard Noa shouting from the kitchen.

The boy mumbled something underneath his breath as he continued climbing up the stairs, avoiding eye contact with me.

'Rajab, we have a new boy staying with us here . . . His name is Arman.' Noa rushed to the living room, her right hand pointing at me sitting quietly on the sofa in front of her. I could sense a hint of excitement in her voice, expecting Rajab to share that. The boy stopped almost at the top of the stairs.

'I'm tired, innit,' he mumbled, before calling back down the stairs. 'All right, maaaaate.' I could barely recognise his accent and realised he was putting on a local one.

I heard his feet on the last couple of steps, then a door slamming behind him.

Noa, still standing in the doorway, was clearly confused by his reaction, mumbled to herself.

'What are ya like, Rajab?' She then looked at me with a visible hint of confusion and embarrassment on her face.

'Sorry, Arman. Not sure what's got into him. He's usually much more friendly than that,' she muttered after a confused pause. 'He must've had a long day at school or summat.'

I was already thinking of moving on if that was how Rajab was going to act.

I already imagined how the conversation with Julie would go at the end of the week. Then I heard the door opening and a boy's voice.

'I could have scored twice, if Adam had just passed the bloody ball, like literally he never passes . . .' And then a boy of eight or nine came into the living room, wearing a football kit, with football boots around his neck. He smiled immediately when he saw me.

'All right, mate,' he said and held his hand up so I high fived him, unable to keep from smiling.

He ran back out into the kitchen, still talking about football and it was as if he had blown away the bad air from the other boy's behaviour. Everything seemed great apart from Rajab.

Noa called from the kitchen. 'Rajab, Ella, Arman, Jared, dinner is ready!'

I realised how long it had been since I had been called for a meal like this and it made me think of home, eating dinner with a family, rather than in a canteen. For a moment I saw my sister eating, laughing, covering her mouth and I squeezed my eyes shut. Ella and Jared came running in and immediately sat in their places at the table. After a while, Rajab came in quietly, wearing a football cap pulled low over his eyes. We sat around the dinner table and Noa brought in plates of food.

'Do you play football?' Jared asked, smiling and munching on his chips, while looking at me.

'A little bit but I'm not very good at it,' I replied.

'What position do you play?' he followed.

'Errm,' I mumbled while my mind rushed for an answer so that I would not come across as completely football illiterate or rather everything illiterate, especially in front of Rajab. It was true I had been kicking a football with other young people in the hostel every now and again, and I had selected GCSE PE as a subject at school, but I still had a lot to learn about specific positions and rules of the game.

'Defender,' I responded without knowing much about it.

'Rajab plays striker, and he's really good, aren't ya, Rajab?' Jared said as he turned sideways to look at him, expecting a response. Rajab shifted a little in his chair, quietly smiling under his cap and chewing on his burger and chips.

'I'm all right, innit, Jared,' he mumbled, his adolescent voice striker.

'Yeah, but you're well crap at the defending, aren't ya?' Jared said, looking again at Rajab for his reaction. I got the sense this was a conversation they had a lot.

'No, Jared, you're crap at scoring innit,' Rajab hit back quickly. He seemed tense.

'Not as crap as you are at heading,' Jared hit back, smiling provocatively.

'No, you are crap, Jared,' Rajab hit back. I could see a visible sign of disappointment in Rajab's tense and spot-filled facial muscles. Jared still looked relaxed, smiling pleasantly and carefully monitoring Rajab's reaction. I could see Ella frowning silently as she was having her dinner. She had had enough of their argument about football already. 'Muuuum! Please tell them to be quiet. We're not interested. No one cares.' She frowned at both of them.

'Will the pair of you be quiet please,' Noa muttered calmly.

'Jared started it,' Rajab jumped in.

'No, you started it,' Jared replied.

'No, you started it,' Rajab hit back.

'I was only joking,' Jared said with a calm smile.

'Yeah, right, Jared,' Rajab frowned.

Despite Jared being half Rajab's age, I could see that he knew exactly how far to push Rajab.

'Arman, you don't have to listen to their ranting about football,' Ella exclaimed, frowning at Jared next to her. It's all they talk about.' She looked sideways at them, frowning.

'What do you like to do in your spare time?' Ella asked. 'Ermm, I-I-I like sports,' I replied uncertainly, not knowing what else to say.

'That's cool. Like what?' she asked after a small pause.

'Erm, I like martial arts,' I heard myself responding, but I had never been to a proper martial arts club before to learn anything about it. I had only heard some names like Bruce Lee from other boys in the hostel.

'That's well cool, Arman,' Jared intervened. 'How high can you kick?' he asked, his eyes lighting up. 'Can you kick up there?' He pointed at the spot near the light bulb positioned right in the middle of the creamy white ceiling of the dining room. Part of me was ready to say yes, just to look cool in front of everyone, especially Rajab, but another part of me hesitated.

'Errm–no, not really. But maybe close,' I mumbled.

'Wow, that's well cool,' Jared exclaimed. 'I bet Rajab can't even kick this high,' he said, holding his hand by his chest while stealing a teasing glance at Rajab with a warm grin on his face. I watched Rajab still chewing on his burger indifferently, as if he hadn't even heard our conversation.

'You can't, can you Rajab?' I heard Rajab mumbling something underneath his breath that got lost in the air. Jared asked again. It seemed Jared and Rajab's chattering would often continue until they were told off by Noa.

After dinner, another row broke out between Ella, Jared and Rajab over the remote control between Ella, Jared and Rajab. I heard Ella's voice: 'Muuuuum! Tell 'em!'

'Tell 'em whaaaa?'

'They're watching football again.'

I went up to my room and read one of the science books from school. I thought of how so many of the answers to the questions I asked as a child were here. But I knew that I could not think about things like that for long without being dragged back into the past.

I thought of Rajab and what he must have seen to get here, like me. How he just wanted to fit in and I thought I understood. He wasn't being unfriendly; he just had his own wall and he didn't want any cracks in it. Here, people were free to talk about their siblings, their parents, their memories and their feelings because they didn't worry as much about what might come pouring out. That's all Rajab wanted – to fit in so well that his past no longer existed. What could be better than that?

13

Second School, Herne Bay

'Where's Bin Laden then, eh? Where's fucking Bin Laden?'

The tall boy was smiling but he was not friendly. Even if I hadn't understood what he was saying, I would have known that. His face was close enough to mine so that I could smell the cigarettes on his breath. His friends were laughing behind him, as he stared down at me. I realised the canteen had become silent, the chatter and movement suddenly stopped. The air felt thick. People were staring at us. I looked sideways at Serenity and Sarah, who had put down their sandwiches, their eyes wide. I swallowed. I had thought a new school would be a chance to start again. To make use of everything I'd learned in the last year.

How could I tell him that men who followed Bin Laden had done so much to my people, my family? How could I tell him about the shouts of Allah Akbar, huddled around the radio?

This time, I understood enough to answer people's questions. There were no thumbs-up and there was no smile. I knew enough to answer their simple questions. Understanding the cruel things they said was the worst part of this. But at least I could defend myself now.

Two of the girls from my English class had asked me to sit with them at lunch on the first day and then again after that. They were friendly and popular, and I sat still, trying desperately not to do anything that stood out. I even found myself relaxing and enjoying it. But less than a week into school and attention was all on me. The tall boy had come over to talk to Serenity, but she had told him to go away and flicked her middle finger up at him. Then he had noticed me. He asked me where I was from and because I felt safe, and wasn't thinking properly, I had told him. That's when he asked his question. Though only a couple of seconds had gone by, it felt like hours.

'I don't know,' I said carefully.

'You don't know?' He was looking me in the eye, nodding. Then he looked at Serenity.

He and his friends started laughing and he walked off.

'Let me know if you hear, yeah?' he called over his shoulder as he walked away with his friends, still laughing. The buzz of conversation started again. Sarah touched my arm.

'You OK, Arman?' she asked.

'He's such a wanker,' said Serenity.

I sat, unable to eat, still feeling everyone staring at me. Not only could I not escape my past, but it also wouldn't even be mine to tell. In their eyes, I was the same as the men who killed all those innocent people. The war was in the news most nights, the search for Bin Laden. At my previous school, some children had brothers and sisters in the army; I was sure some of the children here would too. I wanted to tell them that I understood how scary it was, that I had seen the monsters up close. They were the same monsters who had been killing thousands of my people for decades, but I wanted to explain that this wasn't like football, that we weren't on different teams. Life is always more complex than that.

*

That afternoon I couldn't concentrate. Even in the subjects I was beginning to enjoy for their certainty – the periodic table, the diagrams of bonds in the atom, the rules of formulas in mathematics, the order of things, even when it might look like there was chaos. All I could think of was the laughter. I realised I had been thinking that if I worked hard enough and long enough, if I watched enough and listened, if I read enough books and practised and practised and practised, I could make myself into someone who would fit in.

At home, I rushed straight upstairs and lay on my bed, pulling the duvet over my head. It took all of my strength to keep the wall, to stop thinking about things that would take me back inside it. 'Dinner's ready, kids,' Noa called up. Then a few moments later I heard a knock.

'Arman, dinner.'

'I'm not hungry,' I replied. I felt her sit down on the side of the bed.

'Well come down and sit with us, even if you don't want to eat anything,' she said. 'Please.' I followed her downstairs and sat pretending to eat.

'How was your day today, Arman?' Noa asked.

'Good, thanks,' I mumbled, pretending that my mouth was too busy chewing.

I tried to work out if Rajab was looking at me, but I didn't want to look at him in case I met his eye. I wondered if he had heard what had happened. Maybe he had even been there. I hadn't seen him; I hadn't seen him once yet.

What if this happened every day? What if that was enough for Serenity and Sarah to stop talking to me? Before my thoughts spiralled, I caught myself. How pathetic to be worrying about such small things. Here I was, in a house, in my own room, with as much as I could eat and drink, and with the only thing to worry about being some words. I had survived things far worse. If I did have to do this, on my own, I would do it the same way I had done everything else, one foot in front of the other, even when it felt like I couldn't take another step, until I got to the next place. But I couldn't ignore the weight that pushed down on my chest.

That night, I read school books until my eyes burned.

14

Herne Bay

I licked my lips and cleared my throat nervously.

'Sin from thy lips? O trespass sweetly urged! Give me my sin again.'

'You kiss by the book,' Serenity said with a relaxed smile, looking at me sideways with a grin on her face possibly meaning: *That was easy.*

I sat down smiling, my face hot with relief. A couple of people at my table leant forwards and said, 'Well done.' A few people even clapped.

Only some months ago, I had listened with panic as people had read out loud from this book. It was as if I had forgotten how to speak English all over again. I had kept my eyes down when it was time to read, barely able to follow along on the page. And every night, we would sit around the table and Noa would ask us how our days were. She seemed to know when Ella or Jared were worried about something or when Rajab needed space. Whatever was happening, she was calm. She was calm when Jared got into a fight at school, or when Rajab came home late one night and I heard him shouting. She asked her questions gently, patiently waiting for us to answer. She bought me a bike for my birthday, and I rode it to kung-fu practice.

I had got into a routine of making myself a cup of instant coffee just before going to bed and I then struggled to fall asleep. Sometimes, when I couldn't sleep, I would get up and go onto the computer to read the news or go through some of my school subjects that I thought I was behind in or wanted to get ahead on.

One night, Noa came down and found me. She sniffed my mug.

'How many of those have you had?'

'Two,' I said.

'Well that explains why you're finding it so hard to get up in the morning.' Then she explained that coffee had something in it that stopped you sleeping. I had no idea.

I enjoyed learning new things all the time. When I didn't do schoolwork, I practised kung fu and went for jogs along the seaside in Whitstable. Soon, I realised I was addicted to that pleasant feeling you get after intense physical exercise. I felt more relaxed. More confident and happy.

I came to realise that most of the children at school didn't like school. They couldn't imagine anything worse than school. Being told what to do, not being able to do what you wanted, when you wanted. But I knew there were many worse things than school. If it hurt to practise something in martial arts, or I found something difficult in maths or science, I just kept going. I enjoyed the challenges that came with it. I enjoyed the learning process, of discovering new knowledge about the world. I put schoolwork in that place in my mind for things that you have to get through and I realised that this was not something that most of the pupils at school did. They spent so much time and effort avoiding work.

In English, we watched a film of *Romeo and Juliet*. The class seemed to concentrate on the love story but I was more interested in the two families at war. Two enemies, sworn to wipe each other out. And the children who die because of it. It was like a war. When I said this in class, my teacher Mrs Wilson said it was a very interesting idea and for the first time I had a feeling that I might see things differently to the other children and that was OK.

Since the beginning, Sarah and Serenity were still my friends. They had not abandoned me that first day after the incident in the cafeteria.

When I'd first arrived at the new school, Serenity had been standing just outside reception, her back resting against the wall. She had waved as soon as she spotted me walking through the school courtyard, but my eyes quickly dropped to the floor.

'What time do you call this?'

I examined her face for some trace of doubt but all I found was a smile.

'Come on you, lazy git,' I heard her muttering as I watched her arms opening towards me, gesturing for a hug, her long, thin purple-painted fingernails hanging in the air. I found my body trembling rigidly right in front of her, unsure of what to do now.

'Come on then, you.' I wasn't sure what to do but she hugged me to her, my body went rigid. I could smell her shampoo and deodorant. I had never been this close to a girl before.

Then she was off down the corridor. I wondered what it would be like to kiss a girl, but immediately pushed the thought away.

My life settled down into a routine. I would wake up early and read, shower and put on my school uniform, excited to get to school. Often Serenity would be waiting outside reception and we would head to class together. At lunch I would sit with her and her friends, a group of five outgoing girls who would sit in the lunch hall, laughing and shouting.

Or if the weather was good, we would sit on the benches outside, or sit on the grass, and eat lunch. Sometimes two kids would have a fight and the other kids would run as fast as they could to form a crowd around them.

It seemed as if Sarah and Serenity knew everyone and after a while, people would nod at me in the corridor. People seemed to find things I said funny. Often I wasn't making a joke; I was genuinely confused by something someone had said, a piece of slang, or perhaps something on TV. But slowly, I made friends. It still felt precarious, as if one wrong move would make everything crash to the ground. I still woke from nightmares screaming, my hands cramped from clenching them too tight.

I would to go for a long walk down on the seafront on a Saturday evening and one evening Rajab asked if he could come too. We walked down the hill in silence and then I heard my name shouted out. It was one of my friends from the year above me in school.

'Arman!' they called out. I high fived them as they came up and said hello. They laughed when I said we were going for a walk. Rajab kept quiet the whole time but I sensed him looking at me as we walked along the promenade. I looked out over the darkness and, like every night, tried to ignore the thoughts of those ships out there, rolling on the sea.

'Well done, Arman and Serenity,' said Mrs Wilson. 'A wonderfully passionate interpretation.'

I felt my face go red but it couldn't spoil the moment. The bell rang and we all went out for lunch. It was a sunny day and we were sitting on the field when Tony, who I knew from computer class, asked if I wanted to come and kick a football about. I hardly ever did but I was feeling so happy that I agreed. The girls all waved me away, whistling.

I was about to kick the ball to Tony when I felt a powerful shove in my back and almost fell forwards. It was Mark.

'I didn't know you played football, Bin Laden,' he smiled. 'None of your girlfriends are here now.' His friends surrounded us. They were shoving us together. I tried to walk away, but they kept surrounding me.

'I don't want any trouble,' I said.

'You should have thought of that,' he said, poking me in the chest. I put my hands up, palm out.

'You. Fucking. Bin. Laden.'

He grabbed hold of my shirt and turned to grin to one of his friends.

I grabbed his wrist and twisted it back. He screamed and let go of my shirt but I kept twisting. He dropped to one knee.

'This is called a wrist lock. If I keep pushing in this direction, quite soon your wrist will break.' He was moaning and trying to twist away from the pain, but I kept the pressure on his wrist. His friends had all backed off. I leant in and whispered into his ear, 'You don't know anything about me. Look at me.' He looked me in the eyes and shook his head miserably.

'Do you want to keep this going?' He shook his head again.

He walked away, brushing tears from his eyes, hissing: 'Fuck off' to his friend who asked how he was.

At dinner, Rajab greeted me with: 'All right Jackie Chan,' under his breath and I couldn't help laughing.

'What are you two laughing about?' Noa asked, as she brought the plates in.

'Nothing,' we both said together.

15

Whitstable

I saw the eyes and teeth first and suddenly the bright room had turned dark and there was a roaring sound in my ears. I knew I was awake, but it was as if I was in a nightmare – I could smell unwashed bodies, hear the marching of boots, the clicking of nails on concrete. I could feel the teeth in my leg, shaking me from side to side, dragging me backwards . . . I just stood there, my hand still on the door handle, too scared to move. I had always managed to avoid dogs out on the street, crossing the road and never going to anyone's house if they had a dog. But now there was one in the kitchen. I glanced at the drawer where the sharp knives were kept.

'Arman, is that you? Why are you standing out there? Come in and meet Teddy.' Noa was smiling broadly.

My chest felt tight and I could feel my heart beating quickly. The dog barked and it took all my strength not to turn around and run away back upstairs, to hide under the duvet. I suddenly needed the toilet urgently.

'Come in, come in, you're scaring him.' Shaking my head, as if from a dream, I walked into the room sideways and stood as far away from the dog as I could get, by the back door. Ella was tickling the dog's pink belly and it was wriggling around on the floor in delight, its tail wagging furiously. Now I looked at it some more, it was really quite small. Noa was chopping something on the side and singing to herself. She looked up.

'You OK?' she asked.

'Just tired,' I said. I walked sideways again, ready to jump backwards if it came for me. In the living room, I sat down slowly on the sofa, keeping my eyes on the doorway. Breathing deeply, I felt my heart rate start to slow down. I even started to feel embarrassed. It was a baby really. But still, there was no way I could live in a house with a dog. How could I keep everything behind the wall, with the sound of a dog barking. As if on cue, I heard it barking from the next room. Although, now I listened properly, it wasn't even like a dog barking. The dogs I had known had deep, harsh voices, like men shouting. This dog had a high-pitched yelp, which was mixed in with Ella laughing.

'You're very quiet today, Arman,' said Noa, leaning around into the living room. You sure everything's OK? No problems at school?' I shook my head.

I tried to watch the TV with one eye, the other on the doorway, jerking every time I heard his feet skittering on the kitchen floor. I wanted to go in and tell him that I wasn't afraid of him, that I had dealt with far scarier animals than him. But the thought of getting near to him froze me to the sofa. When Rajab arrived, I put my head around the door to watch how he reacted but he seemed fine, reaching down and giving it a scratch. Whatever he had experienced, it clearly hadn't involved dogs. Or maybe he was just better at hiding it than me.

That evening, after dinner, when everyone went into the living room to play with the dog, I said I had homework and went up to my room. I sat reading my science and maths books until I heard everyone go to bed, then I crept out into the hall to listen. Nothing, just the usual sounds of the house.

Having the dog at home gave me more of an excuse to leave early and stay late at school. We would have exams in a few months and there were classes for pupils to practise with mock exam papers. I had never sat an exam before, so I went to all of them, practising over and over again how to read the questions and how much time to take. It got so the teachers made a joke about it. 'Arman, you don't have to come to all of them!' For most of the other students, schoolwork was something they did instead of things they'd rather do but for me, it felt imperative. However, I had to go home sometimes, and I found it hard to hide my feelings for Teddy. Noa noticed that I would walk straight back out of a room if he was there and a couple of times, I raised my voice and said that him licking everything was disgusting.

Julie came to see me one evening and we went for a walk.

'The school are predicting fantastic grades, Arman,' she said as we walked by the sea. I nodded. 'Have you thought about what you'll do next?'

Sarah and Serenity were going to the sixth-form at our school to study Leisure and Tourism, but I'd talked to one of the teachers and he'd suggested that I could take A-levels and even go to university.

'If you get the grades, there's a chance you'd be able to go to a sixth-form somewhere else, at a better school, but it would mean leaving Noa and we'd have to apply now,' Julie said.

I had been dreading this next stage of my education for a while. The thought of leaving my room, Noa and the other kids filled me with fear but the thought of university, of all the things that I could learn, felt so incredible. I wanted to study everything. Every time I learned something, it pointed towards ten more things and there was so much I had no idea about: philosophy, religion, science, mathematics, literature, technology. I had spent so long using my brain only for survival that it was starving for knowledge. If you made yourself useful with so much knowledge they could not argue that you were low skilled, that you weren't contributing. When it was time to fill in a form and you could demonstrate, in perfect English that you were one of them, then you belonged here.

'We can do the application, I guess,' I said.

'Brilliant,' said Julie, looping her arm in mine. 'In the meantime, we just need to work out what to do about you and that dog.'

After my conversation with Julie, things gradually improved. She had clearly spoken to Noa, explaining my anxiety around dogs, and Noa made a real effort to keep him away from me. I was still on edge when he was around but I came to see that he was not like the other dogs I had known. He was treated with gentleness and kindness and was gentle and kind in return. He would roll around with Ella and Jared and never came close to biting them. Gradually he stopped being a part of the past and started just being part of the house. I stopped watching him every moment.

One night, while we were all watching a film, without thinking I reached down and stroked the top of Teddy's head. His fur was soft. Ella watched me, smiling.

As the exams approached, I revised even harder. Suddenly, it felt as if everything before had been leading to this moment. I just had to get the results I needed to go to the sixth-form at a grammar school. It was the next step I had to take. The next place I had to go.

16

Sixth Form, Maidstone

The second time I moved after leaving Noa's house, in Whitstable, I was living on my own for the first time. It was a low, dark house on the edge of an estate in south Maidstone, the walls had deep cracks and the garden had an abandoned fridge in it. The house smelt of damp as I opened the front door, and there were letters piled up behind the door. I dumped my bag and went from room to room, imagining what Noa would say as we walked round the house. She would tut at the broken tiles in the bathroom and the mouldy shower curtain, and fiddle with the hotplate in the corner of the bedroom, which was all I had to cook on. I pictured her opening and closing a cupboard, wiping a hand over the greasy surfaces.

'On the bright side, Arman, you don't need to buy any furniture,' she would say. 'Because there's no room for any.'

I looked out of the window at the flat white sky.

'At least there's no railway,' I said to myself, sitting down and smiling into the silence.

I thought for a moment of my previous flat in Tonbridge, with Ehsan singing as he stirred a pot of red beans or lentils that he'd brought back to the flat in huge bags from Lidl. Every few minutes the windows would shake as the trains went past. When Noa had dropped me off, her eyes had been red-rimmed as she said goodbye, hugging me tightly. Ella waved from the car.

'And make sure you've always got credit, in case you need to text or call me, yeah?'

I had closed the door to the street and stood in the hall, my eyes screwed tight. Suddenly I wanted to open the door and chase out after her, get back in the car with her and Ella, back to my room. To listen to Jared and Ranjab bicker. To be in the middle of the raised voices and the crying and the laughter . . .

But I had been so sure that I was ready to be on my own. She had told me that I didn't have to go, but I had insisted.

Rajab hadn't come out of his room to say goodbye. He just called out: 'Later, mate', his voice muffled. We had never spoken about the past but I would miss our silent walks down by the sea. Sometimes I would catch him looking into the distance and something about the look of effort in his face would feel familiar.

The programme for getting me accommodation and pairing me up with Ehsan was called 'finding your feet' and I realised that again I was going to have to put one foot in front of the other, even though I felt I couldn't.

Ehsan and I had spent a whole week cleaning and painting the flat that August, then I tried to find a job to save money before school started. I spent my last £40 on a baggy blue suit and black tie from Matalan.

But after a month of taking the eighty-minute journey from the flat in Tonbridge to the sixth-form school in Maidstone, I realised the £40 I was receiving from Social Services to cover my living expenses was not enough for my bus and train fares, never mind food, clothing or supplies for school. I would get back to the flat exhausted and try to read in the kitchen, while Ehsan teased me.

'You should sell some of your books, and then you would have money for the train.'

However, I had no choice but to move somewhere closer to the school. After a couple of months searching and waiting, my new keyworker, Alison, found me an empty two-bedroom house on the outskirts of Maidstone, which was a thirty-minute bus ride to the school.

When I had revealed the news that I was moving to Maidstone to Ehsan, he looked at me, frowning. He insisted I should ask Alison for extra money to cover my transport costs or search for other ways to fund my travel fare, instead of moving away. I explained I had already exhausted every idea I could think of and that I had no choice but to move closer to the school.

'Whatever you want, man,' he said, before disappearing to his room upstairs. After that day, our strolls along the high street, evening conversations, and loud music stopped. In the mornings, I would wake up early for school and would stay late after school in the library. In the evenings, I would hear him coming back, clattering pans before disappearing into his room, quietly. I missed the noise and the smells of cooking, the music he turned on everywhere he went.

I took out my phone but didn't want to bother anyone and had so little credit left as it was. It was hard for me to connect with people. There were so many I had left behind. I found that keeping a distance between me and other people protected my heart and prevented me from feeling any more loss – I didn't think I could withstand any more.

'So bloody tired this morning,' said Richard, theatrically yawning. Then, when no one responded. 'Last flight out of Lisbon, probably not the best idea.'

ACROSS MOUNTAINS, LAND AND SEA

Richard was tall and blond and played rugby. That description applied to a lot of the boys in the sixth-form school. Eventually one of the other guys cracked and asked him why he'd been in Lisbon. This was enough to start a conversation about other European cities that people had visited and what they thought of them. I listened with one ear as I checked over an essay I had written, marvelling again at the confident ease with which they approached life. Cities were like a list of items on a menu for them to choose from. Lisbon, Barcelona, Paris.

I wondered what Sarah and Serenity were doing now. Comparing what they'd done over the weekend, smoking cigarettes and drinking cans along the seafront, perhaps. If someone had a birthday, they'd go out to socialise, maybe taking the bus to Canterbury. I had only been a couple of times in all the time I'd been in Herne Bay. The thought of casually taking a plane for a weekend trip seemed impossible to imagine. I had only seen planes high in the sky. I wondered for a moment what would happen if I talked to them about how I had travelled in the backs of trucks and underneath lorries, but I rammed the thoughts back down. It was a dangerous path to go down. In the six weeks or so I'd been at the sixth-form, I had fallen back into silence, not because I didn't understand what was being said, but because I didn't know what to say or how to talk to the people there. When they talked about what they had done for their weekend, how could I reply that I had moved from one dingy flat to another one, so that I could afford to come to school and eat. How could I explain I barely spoke to anyone the entire weekend? I would sit for the thirty minutes of registration desperate for it to end so I could go and begin classes. I had slowly got into the habit of spending time before and after school in the library. At Herne Bay, you were strange if you went to the library. Kids would get called names. Here,

117

pupils as young as twelve would come to the library to pick up books, or discuss their studies, like adults.

After a few weeks, I noticed I would often be sitting opposite the same girl in the library. She had brown hair and blue eyes and would be listening with headphones as she read. A couple of times we caught each other's eye.

'Hello,' I said, extending my hand to her. 'I'm Arman.' She took one headphone out, looked at me holding my hand out and smiled.

'Hi, I'm Aila,' she said.

'What are you studying?' I asked, gesturing at her book.

'Classics,' she said. I didn't really know what that was but I nodded.

'How about you?' she asked. I held up two books.

'Philosophy. And Physics.' I then put the books down and picked up two more. 'And Sociology and Computer Science.'

'Random,' she said. I smiled.

'I guess so.' She nodded and went to put her headphone back in her ear. It had been so long since I'd had this sort of conversation with anyone and I blurted out, 'I was about to go get some lunch from the supermarket – do you want anything?' She shook her head and I mumbled: 'no worries', suddenly feeling foolish.

'Wait,' she said, 'I could do with some air.'

We walked down the hill and from careful questioning, I worked out that Classics was like a specific kind of old history. She spoke passionately about how Ancient Greek and Roman culture was the foundation for so many things in society and had impacted so many things in our history and culture, from politics to the law and art.

I kept nodding, walking alongside her, trying to show that I understood what she was talking about. But, in fact, I had no idea.

'So, why the random mix of subjects?' she asked. I looked at her as we walked. How could I explain that I felt I had so much catching up to do. All the other kids at sixth-form had been in school for more than ten years. They had been introduced to ideas when they were young and had a sense of what they enjoyed, what they were interested in, what they were good at. I had been at school for barely two years and had spent that time learning everything I could as quickly as possible. I hadn't really had time to think about what I enjoyed, or was most interested in, I just had to put one foot in front of the other. The idea of picking one route through and potentially missing out on something important felt terrifying. I had picked my courses so that I could progress in as many different subjects as possible.

'I suppose I just can't make up my mind,' I said, and she shrugged, smiling.

We settled into an irregular routine of getting lunch every now and then. We didn't exchange numbers or talk about meeting outside of school. We only really talked about our subjects but we'd often end up sitting opposite each other and we'd nod or smile. After school though, she would go home and I would go back up to the library.

I dreaded the thought of going back to my cold dark flat alone. Back at Noa's, even when I went up to my room to study, there had been the distant sounds of everyone else below me. And I'd known that if I wanted a break, I could head downstairs and talk to one of them. But in that flat, I was completely alone. I had no money for phone credit, so tried not to call or text anyone. Many nights, I would not speak to anyone from the time I said goodbye to the school librarian to the time I said hello again the next morning. I would lie there trying to read with what felt like a great weight pushing down on my chest. It was getting harder and harder to escape the feeling that something dreadful was going to happen. For the first time since I had left the hostel, in the darkness and the silence I began to worry that I would not be able to keep the past behind my wall. As the days got shorter, I took to wandering around town, watching people Christmas shopping to avoid going back to the flat. There would be couples holding hands and children with their parents. People smiling and excited. I would stroll home slowly, past the river and over the motorway bridge, watching the headlights beneath me. Thinking how in every car there was someone returning home where there would be someone waiting for them. I felt my loneliness like something physical, a dull ache in my chest. I would sit and watch a pan of water boiling, forgetting what I was supposed to be doing with it. I lost my appetite and lay awake, watching the shadows on the ceiling. For the first time I couldn't even delve into schoolwork to escape because I couldn't concentrate on reading anything and didn't know what to do. I could feel myself losing track of where I was and couldn't seem to concentrate.

One Saturday night, a week before school broke up for Christmas, I suddenly found myself in pain, aching all over. I was sweating and out of breath even though I was sitting down. I tried to ignore it, telling myself it would go away. I stood up, thinking that movement might help. I walked around the room, swinging my arms, trying to move the air, to make some noise, to fill the room with something other than silence. To show that I was bigger and stronger than the silent darkness. But I felt suddenly pinned down by the sense of emptiness, the heavy weight of a cold dark night in an empty house on the outskirts of a town where nobody knew me holding me down. The tightness around my chest got worse. I could hardly breathe and I started to panic that I was really ill. I rushed to the front door and opened it to let the fresh air in, gasping. Above me, I saw stars glinting. *The universe is bigger than this. The darkness will not go on forever. The dawn will arrive, and I will make it there. Things will be OK.* I thought of all the nights I had looked up at the stars thinking something similar. I knew full well that even in the morning I would still be here in the cold, in pain, and alone in this empty house. In the following week, school would break for Christmas and things would get even worse as I wouldn't be able to go to the library at school. I had no money to go and see anyone and they would all be with their families for Christmas. I stood, trying to breathe deeply, watching my breath as I breathed out and the cold air gradually brought me back.

I felt slightly better, relieved, feeling less pressure on my lungs. I went inside and drank a glass of water. But as I was preparing to go to bed, the pressure returned and I struggled for air again, choking.

What am I going to do? I don't want to die here alone. Who am I going to call? What am I going to do? I reached out to my phone, searching for numbers to call. I found Noa's phone number on the list, paused for a bit, thinking of whether to press dial or not. Then I noticed the time – it was past midnight. *Too late to call her at this time*, I thought to myself. Then I found Ehsan's number and pressed dial. 'You do not have sufficient credit to call this number. Please top up and try again,' the answering machine responded. I left the phone next to me and tried to take some deep breaths, to relax. But now the realisation that I was not able to even call and let anyone know about my situation made things worse. *What am I going to do?* I tried to stand up to walk around the house again, hoping to shake up the pain, the fear and take some deep breaths, but I felt the weight of the entire world pushing down on my chest with full force. I could not get up, and my breathing was getting heavier. I reached for my phone again and dialled 999. After answering some questions about what was happening, they said I should go to A&E to get checked out, asked me if there was anyone who could take me there and I said no, feeling ashamed. The woman on the phone had a kind voice. As she asked her questions very calmly, I felt the tightness in my chest loosen a little and I was able to breathe more easily. She asked if I would like to stay on the phone with her until the ambulance arrived. I realised this was the longest conversation I'd had with someone who wasn't a teacher in months. Every few minutes, she would check in and I would respond. I must have fallen asleep because suddenly I was jolted awake by someone knocking on the door and when I opened it there were two paramedics holding bags. I invited them in, apologising for the trouble and asked if they would like a cup of tea, hoping they would say no as there was no milk. They asked me the same questions that the women had asked me on the phone and took my blood pressure. I was feeling much better and one of them looked at me.

'There's not anything urgent wrong, as far as we can see here. But you should make an appointment with your GP as soon as possible.'

I was exhausted by the thought of filling in forms and explaining my circumstances. Of getting my keyworker involved. I had never been able to get rid of the feeling that if I was too much trouble, if I took too much time and effort, I would flash up on a screen somewhere and they would decide it wasn't worth letting me stay. But I was also scared and felt like something was really wrong. I was just about to ask if I could come with them when the other paramedic answered a call on her radio. Then she appeared in the doorway.

'Well, see your doctor, get some blood tests.' I nodded and saw them to the door. As the door shut, I felt the air thicken in the room again. I filled my bottle of water and went upstairs to my bedroom, and tried to sleep.

The next day, I couldn't get out of bed and stayed there all day and night without eating anything. I was dizzy, with a headache, and I felt weak and nauseous.

On Monday morning, I tried to get up to get ready for school. I was excited at the thought of being around people. I managed to shower but had no appetite. I hadn't eaten since Friday and had no energy or motivation to leave the house. I just sat on my bed staring at the wall.

I got back into bed and pulled the duvet over my head and closed my eyes, hoping that I would start feeling better soon, so that I could focus on my studies. I slept throughout that day and night, moving in and out of dreams. It was as if a dam had burst, and the thoughts and images I had spent so long trying not to think about came tumbling out. The faces of the dead called out to me and I just gave up. I was lost, a tiny boat tossed about in a huge sea. At times I didn't know where I was. There were shadows dragging their useless back legs across the bedroom floor. I heard babies crying. An old man begging for water. I was back in a truck, being slammed from side to side. I heard the voices of so many people mixed together, like Reza telling his stories of massacres, Kazim practising saying 'good evening'. I was running down a long tunnel towards the light that never got any closer. I was lying on my back in a dinghy, the water just about to break over the edge of the boat and pull me down into the darkness. I held onto my duvet as tightly as I could until my fingers and arms burned with the effort.

The next day, I tried again but was too weak to get up and so I pulled the duvet back over my head. I sent Noa a message wishing her a happy holiday and explaining how much schoolwork I had to concentrate on. I then let my phone fall onto the floor. She had invited me to spend Christmas with her but I didn't have the money and I was too embarrassed to ask her for it. She had said I wasn't ready to be on my own but I hadn't listened to her – I was too proud to admit she had been right. My phone buzzed once but I didn't look at it.

For a couple of days, I left my room once or twice to refill my water bottle before returning to bed. As a few days passed, getting out of bed became harder and harder, and by the end of the week, I no longer bothered getting up any more and remained underneath the duvet inside the freezing cold house, through Christmas Day and New Year, alone. All I had to eat were crisps and biscuits. I couldn't stomach anything else.

A couple of days after the new year, I dragged myself out of bed one evening and found my phone. It was off. Its batteries were dead. I charged it and turned it on. I found several missed calls and voice messages. On New Year's Eve, I had received some messages, including one from Noa and from Ehsan. A couple of hours later that evening my phone started vibrating, ringing and I answered: 'Hello', my voice cracking. It was Ehsan. We'd only exchanged a few messages since the summer, as he was still annoyed at me for leaving the flat.

'Are you OK, man?' he asked.

'Yeah, man, I'm OK. Just a bit sick, that's all,' I whispered back.

'What's wrong, man?' he repeated.

'I'm just sick. I can't speak any louder, sorry,' I whispered.

'OK, man, I'll be there tomorrow,' he said before hanging up the phone. I went back to sleep. The next day, Ehsan came for a visit. He was shocked at what he found and went through the house looking for food. That night he sat over me and made me eat the lentils he cooked. We didn't talk. He just sat near me as I sat with a duvet wrapped around me.

'You need to call somebody,' he said. I couldn't speak and just nodded.

A few days later, my keyworker Alison came to visit, and she accompanied me to the doctor. The GP performed a series of tests and assessments but found no life-threatening health conditions except a bad flu gone wrong. He suggested I should take some painkillers, rest, eat and sleep well. But despite the doctor's reassurances, my symptoms didn't get any better, and I continued to complain to my keyworker about the same symptoms. She made another GP appointment for me. After a couple of repeated appointments and tests, the GP asked if we could speak in private. Alison stepped out of the office. The GP, a chubby and kind-looking man, cleared his throat and repositioned himself a couple of times on his chair before asking if I or anyone in my family had any symptoms of depression or anxiety in the past.

'Excuse me?' I asked, leaning towards him, staring at him in surprise.

'There is nothing to be worried about. Many people experience both at some point in their lives,' he responded calmly.

'I–I mean, what do you mean by that?' I asked, looking confused.

'Well, some of the symptoms of depression and anxiety include appetite loss, lack of energy, sadness and feelings of emptiness,' he said. After listing a few more symptoms, he then paused, his dark round eyes examining mine, looking for a reaction, a response.

'No, no, I don't have anything wrong with me,' I said and stood up abruptly, ready to leave.

'That's fine. I understand,' he said. I didn't want to stay there any more. I wanted to leave. The thought that it would be put on my records that I was crazy was terrifying.

After that day, I returned home and decided not to tell anyone about my symptoms in case they might think I was a crazy person. I didn't want to talk to anyone. I repeatedly ignored calls and stayed in bed for weeks. After missing school for several weeks, the thought of going back to school felt more and more impossible. I hadn't opened a book in weeks. I thought about quitting, but the thought of giving up felt even worse than continuing. At some point I was told that school was aware of the situation and they had offered to help me catch up with the work I had missed. They had said they would come to the house to see me, but I just turned off my phone and pulled the duvet back over my head. I refused to go to the appointments they made for me at the doctor's. I ignored the letters they sent. I lay in bed, trying to sleep but was terrified of the dreams that would come. I felt as if everything I had worked so hard for had been ruined. I told my social worker to inform the school I wouldn't be returning. I felt so guilty about letting everyone down.

As the weeks passed and the days got brighter, I found that I could get out of bed. I took a walk to the local shop. I bought some beans and cooked them, but it exhausted me and I went back to bed. But very slowly it started to feel as if I was waking up from a deep sleep, or coming in from the cold. I started going for walks in the morning and felt the sun on my face. The blood returned to my limbs and I started to feel things again. Ehsan would call me every couple of days. I opened some of the letters, looked at the missed calls and messages on my phone. For the first time in months, I bought phone credit and replied to some of the messages. I looked at the school books in my room and I knew I couldn't do the same thing again, but I felt for the first time in a long time that I could do something. I called Alison and when she asked me what I wanted to do, I said: 'I need to move.'

17

Canterbury

'Allas, my wyf! And shal she drenche? Allas, myn Alisoun!
 (Help! Water! Water! Help, for Goddes herte!)
 Allas, now comth Nowelis flood!'

Some of the class laughed but a lot just looked puzzled.
Slowly Mrs Hunt began to take us through what was happening, translating the middle English word by word, line by
line, into contemporary English. It had been like Shakespeare
all over again when we'd first started to read Chaucer. On
one level it felt good to puzzle though these stories that my
classmates could understand as well as I could. We were all
starting from the same place of unfamiliarity. But bit by bit,
slowly, these stories told by pilgrims walking on a long journey
to Canterbury began to come into focus. Something about
them made me think of stories from my childhood. I thought
about the stories that we tell ourselves and each other and
how they explained the world to us. The fact we were reading
them just behind Canterbury Cathedral, where the pilgrims
had been heading all those years ago, only added to the sense
I had of how much the present was woven from the past.
I thought again about how differently my interpretation of
these stories were. Of these people who needed to take a long
journey, to travel far away from home. Of how my reaction

to the first thought of a man building a boat to survive a flood was not to laugh.

I had been in Canterbury for just over six months, in a house half an hour's walk away from the college. I was sharing a flat with Rajab from Noa's place and one of his friends, Mahmood. They had both ended up homeless after leaving care but Social Services had grouped us together and found a three-bedroom house in Canterbury. It was a small room but it felt filled with sunshine. I was working as a customer service assistant at a local supermarket. I had even met a local girl called Tanya and we had begun to see each other regularly. We would sit in the cinema and hold hands.

As well as English Literature, I was studying Law and Economics, and I was starting to see different stories there too, starting to understand the long histories of how to organise society, so that the weak were not crushed. I had not spoken to anyone explicitly about my past, but I had come to see how my past had shaped me and gave me a unique perspective on issues. Often, what just seemed like some words in a book to them, a theory or an idea, something abstract, spoke to an experience I had lived and emotions I had felt. I came to see how a lot of the books we were studying in English were about this too, and I came to feel comfortable speaking about how I interpreted them. The teachers didn't shut me down, and the other students listened and engaged. I came to see that school could be more like a conversation, rather than me putting so much effort into not standing out, not tripping myself up, that I could bring parts of my past into the light and that it wouldn't overwhelm me. There were still flashes of things that I could not face, moments when something would surprise me. But from the start of term in September, and as the winter came,

I didn't feel that tightness in my chest. My days were full of conversation, at college and back at the house. Sometimes I would think of the dark silent flat in Maidstone and feel grateful that I was in such a different place now. I couldn't believe that I had ever been in a place where I couldn't get out of bed.

One cold night, a few weeks before the Christmas break, I was just finishing watching a film with Mahmood and Rajab when my phone started ringing and 'private number' flashed up.

For a moment I thought about not answering it but then I made a face to Mahmood and Rajab and went out into the hall, pushed the button and held the phone to my ear. I could hear the sound of someone breathing and the sound of running, the crunch of dead leaves under feet. I didn't say anything, just waited, my heart beating.

'Aloo. Aloo. Aloo. Aloo.' I heard a panicked voice trembling at the end of the line. 'Alooo, is that you, Arman?' The voice was so loud it sounded distorted and I had to hold the phone away from my ear. The voice sounded familiar but I couldn't work out who it was. Then there was just the sound of someone breathing heavily, as if running as fast as they could. The clear sense of urgency and panic frightened me.

'Arman, Arman can you hear me? Can you hear me? Please answer me. I need help, please,' the voice pleaded.

'Who is this?' I croaked.

'You don't remember me?' he said. I sensed disappointment in his voice.

'I'm sorry,' I said, listening hard to catch his name, so I wouldn't have to disappoint him even more.

'It's me, Nabi, remember?'

I had a sudden flash of him: curled up on the sofa with his curly red hair. We hadn't spoken since I'd left the hostel but I'd heard the odd thing about him from Ehsan and Ali.

'Of course, man,' I said quickly. 'I remember you. It's just that you sounded a little different,' I mumbled, feeling the heat on my forehead. 'So, ha–how are you?'

'Man, I don't know what to do. Ca–can I come to yours? Wa–what's your address?'

I looked at the clock on my phone. It was almost midnight.

'You – you're more than welcome to come, but I don't think there's a train at this time of the night, is there?' I asked. 'Is everything OK?'

'Man, right now I'm live on air. I can't talk to you.' He sounded proud. 'Everyone can hear me live on air right now. All TV channels, the entire world can see me, hear me, the entire world.'

'I don't understand,' I said.

'They're all after me. Everyone.'

'W-w-why are they all after you? Who are they?' I asked.

Mahmood came into the hall with a questioning look on his face and I waved him away.

'I told him to leave me alone. I told him too many times to leave me alone. He didn't. He didn't. He followed me everywhere. He didn't leave me alone.' Nabi's voice broke on the other end of the line, as if he was crying and shivering.

'Who?' I tried to ask again, but he wasn't listening to me.

'He followed me everywhere. So I killed him.' I felt the dread in my chest.

'W-what? Killed who? What do you mean, man?' I heard the film stop in the other room. 'Man, what are you talking about? You killed who?' I asked again.

131

'My grandfather. I killed him.' He was shouting now.

'When? Why? What happened?' I mumbled. I wondered whether I should be trying to record the conversation somehow.

'I killed him last night . . .' he paused and I could tell his mouth was dry. I could hear his heavy breathing, panting, as if he was being chased. I held the phone close to my ear, holding my breath.

'What do you mean?' I finally asked.

'I buried him there. In the back garden.' I could sense a strange sense of relief in his voice. I could hear his breath and the rustle of the autumn leaves.

'It was his own fault. I told him to leave me alone. But he didn't. He should've left me alone, a long, long time ago.' His voice appeared again, shivering, breathing hard in the freezing cold.

'Man, what's happening? Where are you now?' I asked. He shouted as if I should've known already.

'Can you stay calm and tell me what's happening?' I repeated.

'I can't!' he barked. 'The cars – they're looking for me, chasing,' he hissed.

I didn't know what to do. Whether to call the police. The thought of him alone and scared, whatever he'd done, made me want to look after him somehow.

'Please, please, I need a place to stay, please help me. It's so cold here.' His voice was shivering with fear and cold and he was barely able to form the words.

'Man, I–I'm not sure if that's a good idea,' I whispered.

'Whaaaaat?' I heard him responding immediately.

'Running away from the police is not a good idea.' I pushed the words out of my mouth, feeling guilty.

'So, what sho–should I do?' His voice was cracking.

'Well, you could either go to your nearest police station if you wanted to or just call 999 and explain your situation to them. Whatever has happened, it has happened now. But running away from the police won't help you.' The phone went silent except for the sounds of his footsteps in the leaves.

'Hello?' I muttered, listening carefully. The silence continued as I kept listening. 'Nabi, are you there, man?' I asked again.

'Can't do that,' he hissed suddenly.

'Do what?'

'Go to the police!' he barked.

'Man, whatever has happened, it has happened now but running from the police will just make things even more complicated for you.'

'You don't understand. They're all after my . . .'

'Your what?'

'After my brain,' he said, his voice cracking.

'What do you mean?' I asked, even more confused now.

'The scientists are after my brain.'

'Why?'

'They want it for experimentation.'

'Man, I don't understand what you're talking about.'

'The scientists are after my brain. They want to take my brain out of my skull for experimentation. What's so difficult to understand about that?' His voice was suddenly patronising, as if I was being wilfully stupid. 'They want to compare my brain with the brain of Albert Einstein, Isaac Newton . . .' He said a few more names I didn't recognise but who I assumed were scientists. 'Man, right now, everything I say is being broadcast live on TV, everywhere. I can't talk to you any more, byeeeeee.'

He hung up. I remained puzzled, confused, mouth open, eyes staring at the wall. Mahmood and Rajab put their head around the door and were looking at me in disbelief.

'Man, who was that? Mahmood asked, still holding the remote control.

We sat back down in the living room and I explained how I knew Nabi, told them how we used to do our homework together. I told them what he'd said.

'The last thing I heard he was placed with his foster family somewhere by the sea or London. He was all set on going to university . . . I need to call him again to check what's happening with him,' I said.

I rang him until he finally answered. He was still walking and I could hear his teeth chattering.

'It's me again,' I said calmly, gauging his reaction.

'Yeah, I know,' he said, sounding disinterested.

'So, what did you end up deciding?' I asked.

'I'm not calling the police. I don't trust you any more. Please don't call me again,' I heard him shouting before hanging up again. I called him again, and he answered the phone without saying anything.

'Man, I'm sorry, but you can't just walk all night in the freezing cold in the park. How about Social Services or the hospital? I'm happy to call them for you, if you want me to?'

He went quiet, still walking, saying nothing.

'Please call someone and tell them I've killed my grandfather,' he said after a long pause. I remained speechless as Mahmood and Rajab stared at me, their eyes rolling in shock. 'Oh, one more thing – tell her that our wedding is off too!' he barked. Now I was even more careful not to ask too many questions, but I couldn't help it as he kept dropping new bombshells.

'We can sort all that out if you either go home or go to the police before you freeze yourself to death tonight. You just can't continue walking outside in the park in the freezing cold. You will freeze to death,' I heard myself mumbling on the phone.

'So, you have her number?' he whispered. I could sense his tone changing.

'Oh, no I don't. I don't know who or where she is and certainly do not have her number,' I responded quickly, but it was already too late.

'But I'm happy to call her or anyone else you want me to call if you give me their numbers,' I corrected, as I held my breath.

'No, no – you have her number. You do. You're hiding something from me. I knoooow.' He stretched his voice. 'You've been talking to her, right?' he said. The more I told him to go home or to the police, the more he started accusing me of being in contact with his uncle's daughter, a distant cousin who was supposedly his future wife. Eventually, as his tone became more and more threatening, and any offer to help was shot down, I got fed up with him and hung up the phone. As soon as I put the phone down, I looked up at the frightened eyes of Rajab and Mahmood, still staring at me. The TV was still on mute and an eerie silence descended on our shared house.

'Man, I swear, that dude sounds well crazy. What if he comes for you tonight?' Rajab muttered.

'Yeah man, what if he turns up outside the house with a knife, looking for you?' Rajab added before getting up to double lock the front door and the back door leading to the garden, which was only guarded by a fragile wooden fence. I could hardly believe the situation had turned from me trying to help someone in distress to me now needing help, fearing for my safety. I went up to my room. It was a small room with a bed next to the window, just above the front door.

Now, lying on my bed on my back, eyes open, staring into the dark, I wondered what I could do to help Nabi. *There must be something that I can do to help him.* I jumped off of my bed and rubbed my eyes and face to wake myself up. *What can I do? What can I do at this time of night?* I grabbed my phone and called Ali from the hostel. We'd just about kept in touch via mutual friends.

'Hello, who is this?' he finally answered, and his voice got a little softer when he recognised me. But as soon as I started explaining about Nabi, he cut me off and said, 'I thought you had something important to say, bothering me at this time of the night!' He made that *hah!* not interested or rather disappointed sound. 'If I'd known you were going to talk about that crazy boy, I wouldn't have bothered answering you this late at night.' I could sense he was about to hang up. 'Man, it's late. I gotta get back to bed now,' he spat.

'What do you mean, "crazy boy"? Did you already know about him?' I asked.

'Yeah, man. He's gone mad. I'm telling ya. Real bad,' he added.

'What do you mean? How did you find out about it?' I asked.

'Man – just go to bed. You can't help him, no one can. Too late,' he said sharply.

'No, no – wait. Man, it's serious. He might freeze to death in the cold or get run over by a car or something tonight. We have to do something about it,' I insisted.

'Ha, ha, ha, good luck with that, man,' he laughed.

'No, really – why not?' I asked.

'Man, months ago, he invited us to help him prepare for his wedding to his fiancée who he said was his uncle's daughter based somewhere north, but after spending the day shopping, he attacked me in his own house and accused me of having a secret relationship with his fiancée, which was all in his imagination. There was no wedding, no fiancée.

136

Just too many Bollywood films. That's all it is. Too much Bollywood. He has gone mad already, I'm telling you,' he said. Then, as soon as I mentioned Nabi's claim about killing his grandfather, I heard another cynical *hah!* 'Man, he's been saying all sorts of shit lately.'

Ali explained further about the extent of Nabi's hallucinations and imaginations, which seemed to have stemmed from the trauma of his journey to the UK. I remained speechless underneath my duvet, unable to move, shivering in fear. It was one horror story after another. We both agreed that he should inform the relevant authorities about Nabi's situation the first thing the next day.

In the morning, I walked to college with my head still filled with the details of Nabi's story. I kept hearing his voice shaking, thinking of how scared he must have been. Even if none of what he said was true, he believed it was. If you believe a story enough, it becomes the truth.

I told my keyworker what had happened and she said the police might need to contact me, to take a statement. But they never called.

A couple of months later, I heard Nabi was being released from a secure hospital in London. I called Ehsan to suggest meeting up to talk about it. To go and see Nabi.

'I'm not sure if it's a good idea,' Ehsan said. 'He could kill us both with a kitchen knife, you know.'

However, when I insisted, he agreed to visit Nabi with me and offer some moral support, at least. We both planned to stay as alert as possible and to not let him go into the kitchen alone in case he came back with a knife and attacked us.

Nabi came to meet us at the tube station. The first thing I noticed was his eyes: one looked up, the other one down, revealing an abnormally larger white part in each eye. It scared the hell out of me, but I tried to keep my cool as if everything was just fine, normal. I looked at Ehsan next to me. I caught his eye and could see he was tense too.

Nabi was pale and although he'd put on weight, he was still thin and the skin on his face was loose somehow, hanging strangely. His clothes didn't fit properly and he smelt like he hadn't showered in a while. When we got back to his flat, another powerful smell hit my nostrils. I saw Nabi heading to the kitchen.

'Where are you going?' Ehsan panicked.

'To make tea for you,' he responded.

'No, no – no need for tea, we're leaving soon,' I said, adding, 'we just wanted to say a quick hi, that's all.'

'Just come and sit here,' Ehsan added.

Nabi reluctantly turned and sat on his broken chair next to his broken desk. Ehsan and I sat on his wonky bed cautiously, watching his every move. Ehsan looked at the broken cabinet at the foot of Nabi's bed against the wall. I could see he was trying to drag my attention towards the cabinet. But Nabi caught it before I did. He was super alert.

'Yep, that's where he was hiding, so I removed everything,' Nabi muttered, widening his eyes, his knees bouncing up and down uncontrollably. He caught me looking at him and I looked away.

'Yep, it's all those drugs that they've experimented on me. That's what they've done to me.' I could sense the anger boiling up beneath his words. 'I still have to take pills every day and have to report to them about my whereabouts regularly.' He explained how his neighbours had called the police when they saw him breaking every piece of furniture in the house and throwing furniture onto the street in front of the house. 'They're now monitoring my every move, man,' he said. 'It's all fucked up, man. They fucked it up,' he said, turning his palms upward in the air.

'No. No, you're all right,' I murmured underneath my breath, trying to appear as calm as possible.

'Glad that you're feeling better now,' Ehsan said. I could see the tension in Nabi's clenched jaw. He couldn't stop his hands from trembling, even though he held them clutched together in his lap. I could sense Ehsan trying to catch my eye, hinting for us to leave.

'Why are you guys in a hurry? Stay here tonight,' said Nabi. I slowly cleared my throat. 'Man, we've to go – got college and stuff tomorrow but please let us know if you ever need anything.' I didn't feel I could tell him I was preparing for an interview for a university place. We calmly said good-bye and left.

For a couple of minutes, as Ehsan and I walked towards the tube station, we were lost in our own thoughts.

'Man, it's so fucked up innit?' Ehsan broke the silence.

I nodded but said nothing. My mind was still busy trying to process what I had just witnessed.

'My uncle, God bless him, cut off ties with everyone before he lost all sense of reality and took his own life,' Ehsan added.

I looked at him with a hint of embarrassment and said apologetically, 'Sorry, I didn't realise.'

'That's OK, man,' he said.

I thought back to the times we'd spoken on the phone when I was so busy thinking about what was going on in my head. I thought how I'd avoided so many conversations, about family, about childhood, because I didn't want to risk what might be dragged out into the light. How many times had other people needed to talk to me and I hadn't let them. I had met Ehsan's uncle once when he'd come to visit Ehsan.

I remembered an energetic, healthy man in his mid-twenties who had made us all laugh.

'He hung himself from a tree in the park near his house,' said Ehsan.

We both sat on the tube in silence. There was the sudden roar of a train travelling past us in the opposite direction and we both flinched.

'We are now approaching Tonbridge Station,' the voice announced on the train. Ehsan stood up and fisted me on the knuckles. 'See you later, man,' he said before jumping off the train. I sat back in my seat, crossed my arms and closed my eyes as the train continued passing through endless green fields. I had spent the last few months doing nothing but preparing for my final exams. It was like I was clutching onto something in the water, something that would stop me from sinking into the flashbacks and nightmares. But there was nothing more I could do now. All I could do was wait.

I was suddenly grateful that I would be returning to a house full of voices and movement. I thought of the thousands of boys like me that I had sat with, our backs against chainlink fences, who had suffocated in trucks, or slid down the side of mountains, been dragged under trains and trucks, or died with bitter seawater bubbling in their lungs, or were left hanging from trees in an empty park.

18

London

The three of them sat in a row opposite me across a heavy wooden table in a room lined with books. Two men and a woman.

'So why War Studies, why here?' asked Professor Meade. The room was musty and smelt of old books. I thought of the answers to that question I had rehearsed. Of how to demonstrate the research I had done about their university. I was aware that I was taking too long to answer, that this should have been my chance to demonstrate what a good candidate I was. But now I wasn't sure of the answer.

Before this question, I had always been sure of my choice and why I wanted to read War Studies. *Because wars are terrible, because they cause death, destruction and misery, and I wanted to understand its root causes and stop it altogether – once and for all, so no one would ever have to suffer again because of war.*

That's why I had applied to do War Studies – to end war for once and for all. And when I finished this *simple* task, for the remainder of my life I would focus on making the world a better and more just place for everyone. A world without war and destruction. A world without oppression and injustice. A world without hunger, poverty and exploitation. A world without displacement. A world without monsters.

But as I sat there in that room, as I cleared my throat to speak, a little too loudly, as I felt the blood rush to my face, I couldn't find the words to say this in a that wouldn't sound ridiculous. The answer, which had been cooking in my head for weeks, months, even years, suddenly disappeared. Just like that, as if my entire memory had just been wiped out from the face of the earth. I swallowed loudly.

'Take your time,' Professor Meade said firmly, while Professor Armitage gently pushed a small paper-white glass of water towards me on the wide table.

'Here, have some water,' she said as her eyes remained fixed on me.

'Thank you.' I pushed my resistant voice out of my rapidly drying throat. It almost shocked me. After all, I had a voice. For a moment, I thought my voice had disappeared. I wetted my lips again and stole another quick glance at professors.

'I–I want to do . . . war studies, because war is bad, really . . . terrible.' I paused and looked at the professors for their reactions, but their eyes were still glaring at me in the eery silence of the interview room, expecting more. 'It's bad because it causes death, destruction and misery – and . . .' I paused again, thinking of whether that answer would be sufficient, or if I should say everything that I had been thinking about wars for so long. I could feel my heart rate racing faster and faster and my body temperature increasing, starting to release sweat on my forehead. So I kept throwing out anything that had been gathering in my head for a long time with no structure, or simply just random stuff I thought might be the answer. 'I–I want to do this course because I want to understand the root causes of war in the hope of eventually stopping it . . .' I paused again, feeling slightly relieved that I was now talking, at least.

On the inside, I was now getting more and more fired up, itching to say more about how terrible wars are and why we should stop them once and for all. One of the professors made a mark on the paper in front of them, frowning. It was clear what I was saying wasn't the right thing to say.

'Yes, yes, we know wars are bad and shouldn't be happening and all that,' said Professor Meade, 'but why do you think you're the best candidate for this course?'

I was now running out of all the valuable information I had gathered or had read online about wars in preparation prior to this interview and I was getting as frustrated as the professors facing me.

'Why am I the best candidate for this course?' I mumbled, while my right index finger pointed at my chest and my eyes kept staring in confusion at the professors.

'Yes,' said Professor Armitage in a determined voice, followed by a nod.

The staring professors seemed to vanish as I felt transported far, far away deep into a war zone . . . 'Because I was born in war, I've lived through war, witnessed the misery, destruction and death caused by wars and eventually I fled war. I have first-hand experience of war. I know how destructive wars are and it should be stopped. It should be stopped,' I kept repeating, just like a little stubborn child.

I took the glass of water in front of me, sipped it and sat back on my chair. What I wanted to do was shout at them that war was not a word, or something that could be contained in numbers. It was a pair of jaws that chewed a family apart. That left you with a piece of your heart missing. I could feel my breath slowing, gradually steadying. Taking another glance, I could now sense the hard iron sheet behind the staring eyes of the war professors' softening.

At the end of the interview, Professor Meade asked if I had questions for them. I looked with surprise and replied, 'Yes, I have a question. Can I?'

She paused, collecting the papers in front of her, staring at me, as if she too had been caught unawares.

'Please go ahead,' she said.

'I was wondering if you could tell me why do you do this – I mean, this course – war studies?' I asked.

She briefly explained, but I cannot remember exactly what she said. She then turned to Professor Armitage on her left, who was still fiddling with those papers in front of him, asking if he would like to add anything.

'Yes,' he said and he began talking about how throughout human history, warfare had existed in many shapes and forms, how it had evolved over time and how likely it was that it would continue in the future in some shape or form. Therefore, from an academic point of view, it was important to research and understand its root cause, its nature, and how it was conducted. He spoke passionately for more than ten minutes about human nature and the nature of war and warfare and how it has developed throughout centuries. He then moved on to explain about the need in the 'market' to conduct research, to study war and warfare, and how their institution was uniquely positioned to lead in this important area of academic studies and how very proud they were to offer such a unique and high-quality programme to their students.

He then turned to Professor Meade. 'I hope I have answered that question. Have I missed anything?' he added.

'No, I think you did great,' she replied.

Throughout his explanations about warfare, human nature, and the changing nature of warfare throughout human history, I was mesmerised by the level of depths and details he provided in answering just one question. I understood only a part of what he said, but I kept nodding anyway as he continued to explain it so eloquently. At the end of the interview, the professors shook my hand and told me that the university would be in touch about the results of my interview and application soon. I left the interview room, but what he told me at the end of the interview had already gripped my mind and imagination, just like his firm handshake.

On the train back to Canterbury I sat back in my window seat, looking out at the green fields and large herds of sheep and cows grazing, as my mind replayed the interview in graphic detail from the beginning to the end. Particularly, what the professor said about war, human nature and the changing nature of war and warfare, especially the comment about meeting the need of the market. I wondered what he meant by the market. *What markets?* In my A-level economic classes, I had learned some stuff about market, demand and supply. I remembered – the teacher would show us a graph with a straight line drawn diagonally across it. He would explain that in a perfectly free market scenario, there is a positive correlation between demand and supply, meaning that the line shows the increase in demand, which leads to an increase in supply and vice versa. I could not work out exactly what it would mean in the context of war and warfare. Would it mean that like in an economic market, there is a market for war? And that there is demand and supply for it? And if that's the case, then who demands wars and who supplies them and why?

Prior to the start of the interview, when I was in the waiting room, there had been about a dozen well-groomed and sophisticated, predominantly male candidates waiting for their turn to be called in for interview. I overheard a group of them sharing interview techniques and talking about why they had chosen to read War Studies. There was one young man among them who wouldn't stop showing off his knowledge of wars and how his father, who was serving in the British army, had already been deployed to several war zones, including Afghanistan and Iraq, and how he was 'contemplating' joining the military himself, but was unsure of whether to join the British army or the Royal Navy. The way he boasted about his knowledge of war and warfare, it was spoken of like it was an ideal career path for young graduates, considering its perks, privileges and job security.

While sitting quietly in the calming hum of the high-speed train travelling across the soft countryside, I couldn't stop thinking of everything that I had experienced as a consequence of war. The more I thought about it, the more questions kept creating and recreating, in my mind: *Why is there a market for war? And if it is the same as any other market, then what sorts of products do the war suppliers supply?*

Now, thinking back to my village in the far corner of the world, buried among layers and layers of impenetrable mountains, nothing else from the outside world could ever find its way to those mountains. No cars, no electricity, no phone, no TV or even books, but there was no shortage of machine guns. Plenty of machine guns had flooded the entire little valley. All sorts of them: American-made guns, British-made guns, Chinese-made guns, Russian-made guns and there were even plenty of Iranian and Pakistani-made guns around. Although people would rarely buy the latter ones. Apparently they had been letting people down on the battlefields. Instead of shooting forwards to hit the target, they had been shooting backwards, killing or injuring the shooter.

I remember among men, and even some children, war, warriors and machine guns were the hottest topics, since there was nothing else to entertain themselves within those hills. Almost everyone had a great wealth of knowledge and expertise about guns and how to operate them and how to fix them like a professional engineer, although those same individuals couldn't make advanced machine guns or deadly bombs that would destroy valleys and villages in a fraction of a second. Almost every household owned at least one machine gun, if not many. They were as cheap as the price of a bull or a couple of goats, depending on where they were made. I thought of the soldiers at the borders with their guns and their heat detectors. Every boot, every baton, every link of fence bought from somewhere. Every war creating thousands of displaced people, every bullet shot at them requiring a replacement.

I thought of my teacher explaining how companies grow, competing against one another to sell more and better products to existing customers and by finding new markets and new people who would need their products. While for phone companies to remain competitive would mean updating their products with better and more advanced features to attract customers, for the weapons industry it meant the continuation of existing wars and creating new wars to keep profits growing. Who would want to buy machine guns and war-related products if there were no wars?

After several weeks of thinking and reading about wars and war studies, I concluded that the intention of the course was perhaps not so much to stop wars but respond to the forces of the market and train professionals with up-to-date knowledge, skills and expertise to conduct wars or better wars, more sophisticated wars. That was not what I was looking for. I was not looking to become a war professional, nor did I want to know more about wars. I thought I already knew enough, had seen enough, experienced and suffered enough because of war. In fact, I was sick of it all. I needed no more of it. I did not even want to hear anything about it any more. Instead, I was looking for something different, something that would lead to reducing wars, ending wars, eliminating wars. Something that would lead to a world free of wars, free of war-related death and destruction. A peaceful world. Not a better war or modern war or more advanced war but no wars. No more wars.

When I eventually received a conditional offer from the London university to read War Studies, I declined it straight away. Instead, I selected the University of Kent to study Politics and International Relations, hoping it would provide a broader option and might equip me with the knowledge and skills to help to strive for a peaceful world. A just world. Where wars didn't have a market value.

Part Three

19

Geneva

I stood looking out at the audience looking back at me. My throat was dry. For a moment it was the first day of school again. I panicked that I would not have chosen the right words. That I had no right to speak. I looked down at my notes and closed my eyes. In the audience were people whose decisions would shape the experiences of those who were forced to leave their homes, particularly children. Those in government, representatives of their countries, charities and non-governmental organizations (NGOs). Those whose voices would shape refugee policy around the world.

I cleared my throat and began to speak.

20

Perth, Australia

For a moment, I stared at the flashing light on the phone as it blinked impatiently. The office was almost empty. Most of my colleagues had already left for a relaxing weekend with their friends and family. My Australian colleagues were always going on trips around south-east Asia; some spent their weekends in Bali, Hanoi or Chiang Mai. People seemed to spend their entire lives outdoors in Perth. Cooking and eating and drinking.

After a hard week, I was looking forward to leaving the office and for a moment I thought about letting the call go to the answerphone. I couldn't do it.

I answered the phone, balancing it between my ear and shoulder as I shuffled papers into the red folder on my desk.

'Hello – hello, sir?' a voice replied. I could hear breathing.

'How can I help?' I asked.

'Erm, hello sir, it's George.' George coughed nervously, clearing his throat. George was one of the carers who looked after unaccompanied minors. Normally he projected an air of confidence and capability but now I could hear he was nervous and scared, which worried me. So far, I'd not had to deal with a call like this, though my colleagues had told me stories. Listening now to the sounds of George's whisper at the other end of the line made my heart beat faster.

'I've got to tell you something, sir,' he whispered.

'Is everything OK?' I asked.

'Well, no, not really, sir,' he replied.

'What is it, George?' I said, trying to make my voice as gentle as possible.

'Well, you know Anwar?' Anwar was one of the cases I was working on, one of five unaccompanied children all in the same house on the outskirts of Western Australia, about an hour and a half's drive away from the office. They had all recently been transferred to mainland Australia on an exceptional basis of vulnerability after having been locked up with hundreds of other adults for several years in an indefinite refugee camp in one of Australia's 'offshore processing centres'. They were being looked after by rotating care workers from another humanitarian agency, which had been subcontracted to manage their day-to-day care. I was still catching up after taking on responsibility for their case a few weeks ago. It was a lot more responsibility, delivering casework services to vulnerable displaced unaccompanied children with complex needs and only a few weeks into the job; I was feeling the pressure.

'I'm worried about him,' George said. Having read Anwar's files, this wasn't the first time someone had expressed concern. 'He has locked himself in his room,' he added.

'I see. Maybe he is sleeping?' I looked at the clock on the wall.

'Er, no sir.' He cleared his throat. 'Before locking himself in his room, he told the other boys that he would rather be dead than carrying on like this,' he whispered.

'How long has he been there in his room?' I asked, swallowing nervously.

'Several hours.' George's voice trembled. 'Sir, I think you have to come. You have to come.' He sounded genuinely worried.

'I'll be right there,' I said.

ACROSS MOUNTAINS, LAND AND SEA

As I left the office, the sun still had a sting to it. I stood and closed my eyes, feeling the sun on my face. I thought of the last couple of months in the UK. How every week I would sit in front of an artificial light machine to try to combat what the doctor called a 'seasonal thing'. How I'd sat in the bedroom a charity had arranged for me so I was no longer homeless, as the job rejections mounted up until I stopped applying. Until I stopped doing anything. It felt as if I had been making false promises to myself all along: if I survive this war, things will be better; if I survive that bullet, things will be better; if I pass that border, things will be better; if I survive this sea storm, things will be better; if I pass my English exams, things will be better; if I finish school with good grades, things will be better; if I complete my exams and go to university, things will be better; if I graduate, things will be better. As I had overcome each of those hurdles one by one, I had begun to imagine myself doing great things, like ending wars and making the world a better place for everyone. But at that moment, I was unable to help myself, let alone anyone else. I was too exhausted to make any more promises to push myself to overcome just that one more hurdle. All the time, just one more. Just one more. As I lay in bed, the covers pulled over my head, I had felt that terrifying familiar darkness.

One evening I called a friend in Western Australia and asked him about the weather over there. It was 'bloody hot, mate' every single day, he complained. I had already made my mind up before he had even finished moaning about the hot weather. When I said something about wanting to visit Australia at some point, he invited me to go and visit him. He even said I could stay at his flat until I sorted things out. I applied for an Australian working holiday visa straight away. When my visa was approved the following day, I used all my overdraft allowance and bought a cheap one-way ticket to Down Under.

As I drove out of the city that Friday evening, people were heading out to bars and restaurants. The sound of laughter and music drifting out. I knew that I had to check on Anwar but I also knew there was very little I could actually do. A phrase popped into my head that I hadn't thought of for years – *the war of all against all*. It was from the seventeenth-century English philosopher, Thomas Hobbes. I'd heard it a couple of months into my time at university, when I had spent more time meeting people and getting to know other students than going to all my lectures. But that sentence caught my attention. I went to the library after the lecture and found his book, *Leviathan*. I also began to find out about him, how late in his life he would say, 'My mother gave birth to twins: myself and fear.' How he witnessed the horrors of the English Civil War.

Something about that description stayed with me and I couldn't stop imagining Hobbes as a little boy born and surrounded by countless notorious armed monsters shooting left and right, killing anyone who got in their way. I wondered, if, like me, Hobbes was always afraid of a war breaking out at any minute or whether he was terrified of darkness and going to sleep. Imagining this Hobbes somehow created a warm sense of bond and friendship between us. Perhaps a shared experience. Until then, I wouldn't know how or even whether I should express my childhood fear of being attacked in the middle of a dark night by an unknown group of armed men, monsters. This chaos, anxiety and fear had dominated my early childhood entirely. For me, it was more than just having a 'twin', it was part of me, I thought.

In *Leviathan*, Hobbes aims to understand the root causes of war and tries to provide an ultimate solution for creating a lasting peace in the world. In the first section of his book, Hobbes explains his account of human nature, describing individuals as passionate creatures with a set of appetites and desires who are constantly fighting with one another for scarce resources. According to Hobbes, even when two men are not fighting with each other, there is no guarantee that they are not secretly planning to kill one another for their property or just out of an aggrieved sense of honour. Hobbes says that in such a constant state of war with another, there is no hope of peace or progress.

In such conditions, there is no place for industry because the fruit thereof is uncertain, and consequently no culture of the earth . . . no knowledge of the face of the earth, no account of time, no arts, no letters, no society, and which is worst of all, continual fear and danger of violent death, and the life of man, solitary, poor, nasty, brutish, and short.

When I read this paragraph, I wondered how accurately he had described life in Afghanistan.

Hobbes suggests that in order to avoid such a constant state of war and conflict and enjoy peace, everyone will have no choice but to voluntarily choose to agree to a social contract with a sovereign authority. So you give up your individual rights to the sovereign in exchange for peace and security.

As I read more, my initial passion for Hobbes cooled, and I began searching for other literature that described a different type of peace. A peace that would not only mean the absence of war but also the enjoyment of rights, liberty and justice.

These words quickly became my new obsession for the rest of my time at university. When I discussed my thesis plan with my academic adviser, he looked at me and said: 'I'm afraid you may need to read the entire Western political philosophy to answer those fundamental questions!' He advised me to narrow down my thesis plan to focus on one particular aspect of the subject.

However, despite this advice, I couldn't help losing myself in the rich literature and works of Plato, Aristotle, John Locke, Jean-Jacques Rousseau, Immanuel Kant, Georg Wilhelm Friedrich Hegel, Karl Marx, Ludwig Feuerbach. Jeremy Bentham's notion of utilitarianism and John Rawls' *A Theory of Justice.* I wanted to understand the notion of a good society, what conditions would allow individuals to flourish and contribute to promoting peace, justice and human rights across the world. A world where everyone, regardless of their race, religion or the colour of their skin would be able to enjoy a dignified and fulfilling life.

At university, I was full of hope for the future and had grandiose ideas of the impact I could have. But now, as I drove through the suburbs of Western Australia on my way to Anwar, I understood things differently. I thought of Hobbes' words again – *the war of all against all.* There are hordes at the gates, who want you, your belongings and your freedom. It's them or us.

I had enjoyed university and all the different people I'd met from all sorts of different backgrounds. I was curious and asked questions. People told me I was friendly. My friends even teased me that I was a 'ladies' man' but I just smiled; it felt like a miracle, to be surrounded by people like this, to have access to the words of so many important thinkers. In my spare time, I volunteered to help disadvantaged young people from so-called underperforming schools in Kent to access higher education. At college, I was elected as the president of the student union and represented over 9,000 students. At university, I got elected to chair student meetings and discussions about various social and political issues and joined the national campaign against the government's plans to raise tuition fees in England and Wales. Having worked both as a volunteer with diverse groups of disadvantaged young people in schools in Kent and having represented the interests of over 9,000 further and higher education students at community college, I knew exactly how rising tuition fees would negatively impact young people from disadvantaged backgrounds the most.

As I pulled up outside the address, it was almost completely dark. George, ushered me in, whispering, 'I managed to get him to come down because I said you were coming.'

I found Anwar lying on his back on a sofa and at first, I thought he was asleep, but then I saw his eyes glinting. There was something about his posture I recognised. It was as if the unbearable weight of the universe was pushing down on him. He was someone who had gone through unimaginable hardships.

I followed his gaze up towards the upper corner of the room to see what was there that he was staring at so hard. I saw nothing. There was nothing. I noticed his gaze didn't even travel that far; it seemed to fade somewhere in the air above him. I sat down next to him.

'Anwar, it's Arman. I understand you must be going through some tough times right now – and I want you to know that I am here to help you if you ever need anything at all,' I said gently. I recognised the tone in my voice, which I had heard so many others use with me before.

However, deep down I knew that he wouldn't really believe what I was saying, just like I hadn't fully believed anyone who had said such things to me. I could tell he was listening to me though, despite him staring into the distance.

I tried to imagine what someone could have said to me to change my mind back then, although if I'd spent years in a holding facility and months watching television adverts telling me that people like me weren't wanted, I would probably feel similar to Anwar. Deep down inside, I knew I was lying to him. And he could sense that. It was not hard.

'But I can't help if you don't tell me what I can do for you,' I said. Still no response. I knew none of this was new to Anwar. Throughout his journey, he had already heard those lines over and over by many people in various uniforms, with various job titles, each one requiring his trust to help him, but all eventually disappearing once they got a statement, an acceptance, a story, a quote . . . leaving him alone, in despair. I paused a little longer, thinking about what else I could say to him to get him to talk to me. For a moment, I said nothing and remained silent next to him. Through the front window, I could see city streetlights shining in the distance.

'It's a nice evening. Let's go for a drive,' I said. For the first time, he moved his eyes to look at me.

'A drive?' he said.

'Yeah, let's get out of here for a bit. Take a look around. I think I saw a pizza place round the corner.'

'Pizza?' he said. Then he shrugged. 'OK.'

As we drove, the streetlights lit up his face rhythmically and I tried to look at him as I drove, waiting for him to talk, but he sat in silence. I needed to start on safe ground, so I considered raising the idea of him seeing someone about his mental health. I knew the statistics on asylum seekers and refugees. They were five times more likely to have mental health problems than the local population and one in three would suffer from serious mental distress, but they were far less likely to receive support. Many did not even know they could get help. The ones who did found it slow coming.

'I tell you, I don't miss the rain in England,' I smiled.

He wasn't listening. He was lost in his memories. I wondered what he was thinking about. Which roads did the ones we were on remind him of? What did he have concreted away behind his wall?

The next safe topic to talk about, I had heard, was sports. I briefly explained to him how I had arrived in the UK many years ago just like he had arrived in Australia and how I found sports an exciting adventure and empowering both physically and mentally. I heard him moving a little. I continued talking about the number of sports I had been involved in. After listening to me silently for several minutes, I heard him making a little noise in his throat. I paused a little, slowing down the car, offering a silent sense of invitation, saying nothing so he could join in the conversation – if he wanted to, of course. No pressure. He gradually cleared his throat again and asked: 'What's your favourite thing that you like to do?' his voice was breaking, as if he had not spoken for a while. A long while, perhaps.

'I like all sorts of sport, but mainly I like martial arts,' I replied calmly, while my eyes fixed on the traffic ahead of me.

'I like martial arts,' he said after another pause.

'It's really good, isn't it?' I said.

'Yeah,' he mumbled.

'I used to go to this karate club in Quetta, Pakistan, before a suicide bomber blew it up,' he revealed.

'I'm so sorry,' I said. *So much for finding a safe subject to talk about*, I thought.

While I was in the UK, I had seen the news of frequent suicide bombings in Pakistan, killing dozens of men, women and children, images of dead bodies wrapped in white fabric at the side of the road. The protests of thousands of people calling on the government of Pakistan to bring the perpetrators to justice.

Gradually, as we moved slowly along, Anwar began to tell me about his past. His parents had fled the Taliban during the 1990s and ended up in Quetta, Pakistan. But when the US and NATO invaded Afghanistan in 2001, thousands of the Taliban's fighters, including its leadership, moved to Quetta, Pakistan too, and they made the town where Anwar's parents lived their headquarters. When they could no longer kill innocent people in Afghanistan, they turned their attention to those living in the same city as them. Once again, they targeted those who dressed differently, those who prayed differently.

Some of it I already knew from his file, some was new information. Anwar's family fled again in search of safety, this time in the back of airless trucks, all the way to Indonesia. And from there they boarded a flimsy and overcrowded boat with hundreds of other people, floating for many days and nights, enduring deadly storms. When their boat finally made land, he found himself locked up on an island with other men and some families for years, far away from the mainland of Australia. Finally, he was identified as a fourteen-year-old vulnerable unaccompanied child at risk and was transferred to Australia for special care and protection. But he was then placed in another prison. This time it was called a Community Detention Program. And his government case manager would constantly remind him they should not get too comfortable in their new detention space and be ready to be removed or sent back to their offshore detention camps at any moment, without warning.

As we were driving back, I was surprised by how it had all come tumbling out. Anwar didn't cry and he wasn't emotional;

he told me what had happened with a flat even tone. I was worried by it and wanted to get support for his mental health, but I was wary. A couple of times, I had made the same recommendation to Abdullah , a thirty-five-year-old asylum seeker I was working with. As soon as he had heard the word mental health, he had lifted up his head, his eyeballs rolling in anger.

'You – you – think I am crazy?' he spat, waving his cup around, spilling his tea. 'Is that what you think? Is that what you think of me? Is that why you want me to visit the crazy doctor? I am not crazy.'

I tried to reassure him that it was his choice, but it was too late. I couldn't really blame him. I remembered how I had responded to the GP's proposal to me to receive counselling. Instead of accepting his advice to receive support, I just carried on as normal and pretended it was all physical rather than mental. There had been times throughout my time at university doing my masters when I had run out of money and had no way of paying for my fees and there was no family I could go to for help. Once again, just as I had before, I spiralled into anxiety and depression. The letters kept arriving, threatening eviction and kicking me off my course. The GP gave me a leaflet about managing stress, which I threw in the bin. Finally, I had been able to secure a loan and hardship payment, which meant I was able to remain on the course. I even went to see a counsellor but stopped after one session. I spent all of my time in the library, desperately trying to make it to my final exams. I just about made it but had to move back to Canterbury and that's where I ended up in accommodation supported by a local homelessness charity. Who was I to lecture anyone about asking for help? I could understand the idea of not making trouble, not giving anyone an excuse to say you were broken, that you were crazy. You would bend yourself into the shape that would let you stay, even if you nearly broke. I didn't want to lose this moment of connection with Anwar.

'Anwar,' I said, looking at him, 'it's not weakness to ask for help if you need it.' He didn't say anything. I took a deep breath. 'People like us, we go through so much on our own. We become so used to losing everyone we know, keeping moving, never stopping and thinking. We know that we are the lucky ones, that there are so many dead, and in camps with no food, or water.' He looked up at me. 'But that doesn't mean we don't deserve help. What was the point of any of it if we don't truly live?' I realise I am grabbing the steering wheel so tightly that my knuckles have turned white. He doesn't say anything, but I see his shoulders lower just a fraction. We pull up outside the hostel and Anwar reaches to undo his seatbelt.

'So how about it? I ask. 'Shall I get you an appointment with the doctor?' He looked at me. 'I can't promise it'll be quick though.'

He caught my eye and smiled despite himself, nodding. I watched him walk up the path and enter the hostel. By the time I drove home, it would be time to go to bed. I wrote up my notes on Anwar. I knew from experience that it would take many more phone calls and emails to try to shake loose any help from the Australian government. It was just the first step of a long journey, but it was a start.

I thought back to that day I received my Master's Degree from the London School of Economics and Political Science (LSE), almost exactly ten years after I had arrived in the UK, completely illiterate. I had never been to a proper school except a few random winter classes before starting year ten at the age of fourteen. And when I finished my master's in the

UK I did not have the money to hire a graduation gown and so I asked to receive my certificate in the post. I had thought it was the end of a journey.

But sitting in the car, I realised it had been the beginning.

21

Greece

At the back of the long queue, I saw a thin woman almost stooped in half wearing a dark blue hijab and holding a broken walking stick. As the crowd surged forwards, her body was buffeted along. I hurried towards her.

'Grandma, can I help you with anything?' I asked politely in Dari. She ignored me. I could see the lines around her forehead and eyes. The queue to collect food was already hundreds long at this abandoned airport-turned-emergency refugee camp on the outskirts of Athens. The noise of hundreds of pairs of lips asking for help, hundreds of hands waving, was overwhelming.

She didn't reply, as my voice seemed to disappear among the roar of the exhausted and hungry crowd while she continued struggling, maintaining her position, and dragging her feet forwards against the crowd. I wondered if she had injured her legs as there was something strange about the way she was standing.

'Grandma, can I help you with anything?' I asked again, this time a little louder. I extended my hand towards her, gesturing to help her step aside from the roaring crowd. 'Can I help you with anything?' I repeated when I thought I had caught her attention.

'Get out of my way,' I heard her mumbling in Pashto, as she continued resisting the forces of the moving crowd around her, who kept pushing into her.

'Speak louder, she can't hear you,' a broad-shouldered man barked in broken Dari before pushing past her, leaving her one step behind, trembling in the disorganised queue of chaos.

I told her I was a humanitarian volunteer assisting refugees and asylum seekers in the camp and offered to collect her portion of food if she would let me borrow her registration document, so that I could go to the food distribution point, instead of her desperately struggling in the queue.

'If you give me your papers, I will get your food and bring it back.' I saw her hesitate, but then she nodded. I watched her right hand searching for her registration papers in her many pockets underneath her hijab while she leant shakily on her walking stick. I saw a child's face suddenly poke out from behind her hijab, and then disappear again. I took the crumpled papers and photographs she handed me and walked to the distribution centre. The papers showed that they were registered with the Greek government as Afghan asylum seekers. The elderly woman's name was Bibi Gul and the child's name was Farzana. She was four years old.

I walked across what used to be a runway, past boys playing volleyball among the rubbish. In the background, the airport building was covered in graffiti with broken windows. All of the signs were still up: 'Domestic Arrivals', 'International Departures'. Several thousands of people crowded in tents and under tarpaulin in the terminal buildings. There were portable toilets underneath the staircase and washing hung on the chainlink fences. There were the abandoned mobile staircases they had driven out to meet the airplanes. If only travelling could be as simple for the people in the camp as it was for the people who had passed through this airport for so many years.

I left Australia after the Liberal Party came into power, essentially declaring war on refugees, with renewed determination to stop the boats while making life unbearable for those who had already made it to its shores.

After leaving Australia, I attended a two-day international conference in Kuala Lumpur that was organised and led by the London School of Economics and Political Science, where high-ranking governments and NGO officials debated the national and international affairs of the region. I was invited by the LSE as a member of LSE alumni. While there, I thought it would be nice to visit a few places in the country but that turned into spending a few months travelling across the region, criss-crossing from one country to another.

I didn't enjoy my travelling experience as much as others did. I exchanged pleasantries with other young people travelling the world and tried to switch off from everything; I tried to experience the world as others did, moving freely from country to country, arriving as a passenger, not as cargo. The airport staff would simply nod and say: 'Welcome, sir.' It was so simple. My burgundy British passport was the key in the door of every country I visited. But after a few months, I felt a kind of sadness. I found myself thinking about refugees like I had been many years ago, more and more, as I sat drinking by a busy road, or walked on the beach. I tried not to look at the news but the so-called European refugee crisis dominated conversation and the media – from sinking boats in the Mediterranean to rising far-right groups demonising asylum seekers. You could see the camps were finding it impossible to deal with the number of people crossing. I saw the shortage of people helping, so I decided to volunteer and help.

I also thought that going to Greece might help me work out where we had crossed in our boat. For years I had tried not to think of it at all, but I had started to think that I wanted to piece it together. I suspected it had been somewhere near

Greece, which had become a key route for those seeking to get to Europe from Afghanistan. All I knew for certain was that my passage had been complete disorientation, with dramatic earth-shattering moments punctuating months of monotonous and uncomfortable waiting. I wondered if I'd be able to understand any more than this.

As I walked around the overflowing disused airport in Athens, I thought of the more than sixty thousand immigrants who lived in makeshift camps, abandoned ports, parks and streets across Greece, as they waited for the asylum process to slowly progress. More than half of them were children. Conditions were overcrowded and dangerous, especially for girls.

I thought about the number of things that had had to happen in exactly the right order for me to be able to walk among them with my little burgundy book, rather than sitting among them. I never really spoke to colleagues about my experiences. I just wanted to be one of them, doing my job.

I walked to the food distribution point to collect the older woman's food. When I returned, I offered to carry it back to their tent for them.

Bibi Gul tried to lead the way up the steep metallic stairs that rose up against the concrete wall to the second floor of the old airport. I could see her fragile body trembling and shivering every time she lifted her feet up the steps, not helped by the child wrapped around her leg. She refused when I offered to give her a hand to assist her climb. 'No, I'm fine. I can walk myself,' she said. I watched her helplessly as she panted and swayed with every step.

'I was fine. I was all fine until . . . it was their death – their death that has crippled me like this – my handsome sons – my lions,' she muttered to me, as she continued to struggle with

167

the child clinging to her. I offered to hold the child so that her grandma could climb with greater ease. The child immediately turned away and pulled her grandma's hijab over her, avoiding eye contact. I didn't insist.

'This is my grandchild, Farzana,' she mumbled as she continued breathing heavily. I looked at the child, who had poked her head back out, and said, 'Mashallah, good girl,' and added 'How are you?' She immediately pulled her grandma's skirt over her face covering the hint of a shy smile.

It took us about ten minutes to climb a dozen or so steps. When we finally got to the top of the stairs, she looked down over at the vast crowd still queuing for their portion of food. She let out a deep sigh. She reminded me of my grandmother.

Moments later, she guided me through hundreds of tiny tents crammed together. This floor alone housed over three thousand refugee men, women and children. The sun was fierce outside but here it felt ten times hotter and more humid with so many bodies so close together. Each breath was an effort, heavy to draw into your chest.

I followed her as she continued zigzagging among small tents filled with children, some crying for food, some asking for a sip of water and others complaining about the scorching, boiling heat inside the high walls, creating an inferno all around them. The sounds of crying babies coming from hundreds of tents: *mama, please water; mama, please food, mama, please, I cannot breathe, it's too hot* continued to echo around us, making it impossible to hear anything except crying. I couldn't help thinking of those rooms I had been in as a child, as people whispered and moaned of hunger and thirst; how their voices were always there, just at the edges of my hearing.

'It's their deaths that have crippled me like this,' she mumbled again, letting out a sigh as she dropped her exhausted body down on a plastic rubbish sack on the concrete floor inside the small blue tent. Farzana crawled out and hid underneath a sleeping bag in the corner. Bibi turned her face upwards and said to me: 'May Allah bring them to justice.' Her hands were held up before her in prayer, her hijab slightly pushed back, revealing her white hair, as she repeated the words: 'May Allah bring them to justice.' I stood up there in front of her with the bags of food, unsure of what to do or even say. I slowly cleared my throat and put the bags down beside her.

'Sit down, *bachem*,' my son. I heard her muttering, her fragile hand gesturing as she shifted further inside the tiny tent. 'I–I really need to go back and help others,' I mumbled, as I accepted her invitation. It would've been rude not to accept her invitation to sit down for a few moments, at least. I sat down on a piece of ripped green plastic placed on the dirty tiles with my legs politely crossed squarely, facing *grandma*, listening to her attentively and nodding without fully understanding what she was saying to me partly in Pashto, partly in Dari.

I reluctantly asked if they had a family member or someone to look after them or help them with collecting their food. She stared at me blankly for a long time, saying nothing as I opened their food packages and spread the food in front of them, regretting my question. I cleared my throat. Farzana had come out. I could tell she was listening to everything we were saying. Every single word. After what felt like a very long time, she said: 'I have no one any more. They killed them – killed my sons – right there before our eyes in broad daylight.' Her wrinkled hands shook.

'Her father, my youngest son, my handsome young man together with his older brother, got shot by the goddamn terrorist – right there, in front of our eyes, just outside our house,' she explained as her voice trembled like her fragile hands.

It was as if time had suddenly stopped, as she became rigid with shock and disbelief. Farzana too was no longer moving.

'Her father and mother got shot in front of our eyes . . . They got taken away from us, just like that – just like that,' she murmured, both her palms turning upwards towards the high ceilings, eyes staring blankly at the tiny space in between nearby overcrowded tents. As she continued describing the tragic incident, I tried not to, but I could picture every detail:

The hot summer wind is blowing into your face across the dry desert on the outskirts of Helmand Province when a group of armed militants armed with rocket-propelled grenades and Kalashnikovs enter your hut, finding your sons, taking them out and shooting them. They do not falter – it is an execution. Your daughter-in-law throws herself onto the wounded body of her husband to shield him, hoping the armed killers may have mercy and stop shooting at her husband, but they shoot her too, right there in front of her four-year-old child. They barely look at you as you wail, begging over their dead bodies.

I caught a glimpse of Farzana's beautiful eyes and her face covered in dirt, and the lines where her tears had run down her face. I could see why she didn't want to leave the safety of her grandmother's hijab. The only one left to protect her. How could she even begin to understand what had happened. She had lost everything: the safety and comforts of her young parents at home, the familiarity of the only land and landscape she had ever known.

'Since then, she has stopped talking,' Farzana's grandma muttered. I sat still, blinking back tears and didn't know what to say but couldn't help thinking how those heartless monsters never had any mercy for any human life regardless of what race, religion or ethnic group they belonged to, not even children. Farzana pulled her grandma's chador over her face, hiding. 'Yes, that's what she does these days, hides underneath my chador,' her grandma said as she gently stroked her grandaughter's head, pulling her closer towards her protectively. 'I'm worried about her. Since we arrived, she has stopped eating too.'

As I looked at her, I knew that hundreds and thousands of children like her had also lost the use of their voice. Even if they could speak, their voices had lost their power. I would never hear their stories. No one would.

As I had done many times over the months, I thought of the photograph of Alan Kurdi that had made global news. The two-year-old boy in his red T-shirt lying drowned, face down on a beach, looking like he had fallen asleep after a busy day playing. I couldn't stop thinking of him in a dinghy like we had been. The waves threatening to tip it over. The sound of their families praying. I remembered how scared we had all been. I knew how the men would have tried to cling onto the dinghy as it flipped over, but the women and the children, in the very cheapest life jackets, which leaked, did not have the strength. Dinghies and floats that were meant to be used in household swimming pools, not on the open sea. The panic, the burning seawater in their throats. Mothers holding their children above the waves as they sank. The strength in their fingers as they tried to reach out to lift them up, to feel their skin. No one would ever know what they called out, what they remembered as they died. No one would know what they had imagined when they held their children up, the futures they saw for them.

They could never have imagined war breaking into their small town of Kobane in northern Syria where Alan lived with his mother Rihanna, but it soon became the frontline of the global war against terror. And thousands of women and girls, just like Rihanna, began heading to the frontline to fight against advancing ISIS militants who had already swept through much of Iraq and Syria, and they were rapidly beheading, maiming and enslaving women, girls and children, including Western journalists live on TV. This was the moment when Rihanna made a difficult decision between choosing to join her comrades on the frontline against armed monsters as thousands of Kurdish women had, or leaving behind everything she knew in the hope of saving her two precious children, Alan, and his older brother, Ghalib. As they travelled from village to village hoping that things in the next village would be different or safer for her little children, they found only destruction. Eventually they had no choice but to cross into Turkey, following many thousands of other families and children fleeing the deadly war. After surviving months with hardly any food or shelter as they fled across borders, they heard about this amazing place of sanctuary in Europe where she might be able to keep her children safe from the monsters, somewhere her children could have bold and beautiful futures. Alan's body would reach Europe, but no future went with it.

For weeks and months, the photos of Alan's dead body on the beach dominated the media. It seemed to cut through and there were discussions about war, conflict and refugee issues at that time. Those of us volunteering in the camp debated about whether anything would actually change. Whether this image would lead to anything beyond social media conversation and lip service.

Seeing Farzana hide underneath her grandma's hijab again, I knew that any progress Alan's image had prompted had fallen short. If there had been any in the first place. Since I had been in Greece, the nightmares that woke me weren't as bad as the day-to-day situations I was facing and the stories of the people I met.

ACROSS MOUNTAINS, LAND AND SEA

'We hope to go to Germany,' Farzana's grandma muttered before adding, 'My son-in-law lives there.' However, what they wouldn't accept is that the borders that had briefly opened had already closed. I said I would come to check on them both in a couple of days, then left their tent. As I started to walk away, the tent immediately blended into all the others around it. When I looked back, I couldn't tell their tent apart from the hundreds that surrounded me.

In the evening, after a long day, I returned to my hotel room in the historic city of Athens, not far from the famous Acropolis. I could see it from my hotel window. I had visited the historic site on a number of occasions; it prompted memories of my university days. I stood by the window, looking out. The city of Athens has always been considered the birthplace of democracy and the cradle of Western civilisation. Whether it was science, philosophy or literature, it could be traced back to here. It was once home to Plato's Academy and Aristotle's Lyceum as well being the birthplace of many ancient philosophers like Socrates, Diogenes and Epicurus. I remembered how every subject I studied at school and university in the UK would somehow trace its origin back to this ancient land. It always fascinated me how and what created such nurturing conditions for such incredible progress, which laid the foundation for an entire civilisation. What could've been those ingredients? Peace? Democracy? Fairness? Freedom of thought and speech? Or something else? I wondered how some societies made such incredible progress while others were left behind, or worse, regressed. Despite the advancements made in Ancient Greece, they also knew war. War was inescapable.

I would think of those people who appeared from nowhere, calling themselves the Taliban, which just means 'students' in Arabic. Between 1993 and 1994 they first appeared in the

mountains and highways of southern Afghanistan, claim-
ing to bring peace and stability in the midst of the death,
destructions and bloodshed across the country perpetrated by
warlords. Some of the people of Afghanistan, who were sick
and tired of the violence and constant bloodshed, cautiously
welcomed their offer to end war and conflict, and to establish
peace and security. As a result, the Taliban quickly rose to
power. In only a few years they quickly captured Kabul, the
capital of Afghanistan, and controlled over 95 per cent of
the country.

While in some parts of the country the Taliban, who shared
important ethnic, language and religious ties, probably did
bring some level of security, in other areas of the country,
populated by other ethnic, religious or linguistic groups, they
brutally annihilated villages, towns and cities overnight and
massacred tens of thousands of men, women and children.
The Hazaras were some of those people.

Arts, music and technology, including TV and music, became
illegal and punishable by death. Books and education, except
religious schools headed by the Taliban Mullahs, were destroyed
and outlawed. Even historical sites like the several thousand
year old Buddhas of Bamiyan were razed to the ground.

It was at university that I read about the history of, the
Hazaras for the first time. I read about King Abdur Rahman
Khan, who was often known as the Iron Amir of Afghanistan
for his absolute brutality and his rule of Afghanistan from 1880
to 1901. I read a historical piece called *Diaries of Kandahar* by
M. Takki Khan. In this document, various British agents report
from Kandahar and Quetta, Pakistan, of the Hazara genocide,
which took place between 1884 and 1905. It included some
proclamations from Abdur Rahman Khan written by government agents who reported that 'it was the intention of His

Highness to exterminate the Hazaras'. Another agent recorded that the king wanted the Hazaras to be 'wiped off the face of the earth'. He had Hazara men killed and imprisoned, women and children made slaves, and he gave their land as rewards to soldiers returning from war.

It was official policy that 'the Hazaras are to be considered as infidels' and 'that the notifications were to be read out in the mosques every Friday'. Mostly this violence was meted out because not only are the Hazara linked to the Shiite tradition of Islam, not the Sunni tradition, but they also cherished their rights and freedom. The Amir sent direct orders to his Commander-in-Chief, instructing him to march towards Hazarajat, with a large army of over 100,000 and 'put all the Hazaras to the sword', stating that 'not a soul of those wayward tribes be safe nor escape and that the boys and girls be taken captive (and made slaves) by every member of the tribes of the Mujahideen of Afghanistan'.

The Amir sent some 350 families of Hazara prisoners, mainly women and children, to be distributed as gifts. These slave gifts were accompanied by further promises of Hazara land, plus women and children, to anyone willing to join the war against Hazaras.

The consequences of the Hazara genocide were as devastating as the king had intended. Over 63 per cent of the entire Hazara population, where millions of men, women and children were ruthlessly massacred, with numerous minarets made out of their skulls erected across the country. Hazara homes were looted and raised to the ground and their land confiscated and distributed to various Afghan Sunni tribes. Hazara women and children were enslaved and sold in a burgeoning trade that was officially taxed and sanctioned by his government. The war lasted for more than seven years and brought the country's economy to the brink of collapse, threatening Abdur Rahman Khan's kingdom. I also learned that if it wasn't for the financial and military assistance, including weapons, money and military advice, provided by the British Empire in India to the brutal Afghan king, it would have been unlikely that the king alone could have committed one of the world's most brutal and silenced human atrocities.

After two failed Anglo–Afghan wars, the British Empire had shifted its strategy from trying to rule Afghanistan directly to making deals with the Afghan king in order to counteract the influence of its long-term adversary, Russia, and protect its interests in the region. The British Empire made a deal with the then Afghan king, Amir Abdur Rahman Khan, to hand over Afghanistan's foreign policy to the British so that he could no longer make any international alliances or treaties with other countries, particularly Russia. In return, the British Empire provided him with large sums of unrestricted financial assistance, sophisticated weapons and other military supplies and helped him build a so-called modern army, capable of protecting the interests of the British Empire in the region. Instead, the despotic Afghan king turned his newly found British-made weapons, money and ammunition against the diverse people of Afghanistan who dared either to look different or believe in anything different from him and his own clan – the Hazaras happened to be both.

The Hazaras were a semi-autonomous and peace-loving people who were governed by different sets of values including women's rights. Hazara women and girls held important social, economic and political roles in the society. They made a significant contribution to arts, music and culture. Hazara men and women worked together, socialised together and even partied together. There were no strong signs of gender segregation among the Hazara before the Hazara genocide in the 1890s. Whether it was in the realms of politics, economics, the military or even in the arts, both Hazara men and women appeared side by side in society. One of these examples are depicted by the monumental statues of the Buddhas of Bamiyan: the male Buddha, Salsal, and female Buddha, Shamama, stood tall together side by side in Bamiyan in central Afghanistan for thousands of years before the Taliban destroyed them in 2001. Shamama, the female Buddha, went down first.

Of course, for a group of men with a medieval mindset and fundamentalist ideologies that treated women not as dignified human beings but as personal property without any rights and freedoms, accepting the Hazaras on any level was unacceptable.

Following his successful genocide campaign, the Amir instructed his entire security forces 'to be on alert' and arrest and kill any Hazaras attempting to flee the country. Apparently, he was worried that if any Hazara successfully got out of the country, they might tell their stories about what had been done to them. Declaring jihad and committing genocide against the Hazaras would give him a 'bad reputation' as he was projected as the moderniser of Afghanistan. The extent of terror he created has never been fully publicized and it continues to haunt all the people of Afghanistan, particularly the Hazaras to this day.

Although in the diaries of British agents, I didn't find a direct reference to the famous tale of Shereen Begum as the leader of hundreds of girls standing against the invading troops, it all made sense now – why as a child I was told those horror stories and why we were so utterly terrified of being attacked, killed or kidnapped at any moment by monsters from behind the mountain, hiding in the darkness, ready to strike. The land where we lived was constantly the prize in a war waged, often by men who believed in beautiful shining ideas and words, often by people railing in the excuse of 'progress'. But only for their people. It was the Hazaras who so often suffered.

One evening when I returned to the hotel from working at the camp in Greece, I picked up my phone and was shocked to see images of dead and injured bodies flooding my entire social media and news feeds. It was yet another deadly suicide bombing. This time it was among a crowd of peaceful protesters in the heart of Kabul. I read the news again and again. The number of deaths and injuries kept rising from dozens to hundreds of dead and injured victims, all of whom were young people, particularly girls: university students, recent graduates, and young human-rights activists who were sick and tired of the injustices, killings (including beheadings) of innocent men, women and children up and down the country by armed terrorist groups as well as the corrupt Afghan government. The explosion happened in Dehmazang Square, in the heart of the capital Kabul, where the Afghan Government had blocked the protesters' route with huge containers to stop them from progressing towards the Afghan presidential palace.

I lay back on my comfortable hotel bed, my eyes filled with tears at the loss of innocent lives, of those hopeful young people who were so determined to fight for peace, justice and equitable development in their country. Since the removal of the Taliban regime from power by Western forces in 2001, millions of young people had been provided with the rare opportunity to attend schools and universities across Afghanistan. A handful of them had even been awarded international scholarships to study at postgraduate level in the developed world. Armed with world-class, Western-inspired education, these young people had returned and joined forces with other progressive young people to fight for peace, justice and equitable development using democratic means like peaceful protests. They had named this movement The Enlightenment Movement, in the hope of finally shedding light on centuries-old deaths, destructions and injustices in the country while laying the foundation for a more peaceful and progressive Afghanistan.

However, at the same time, the dark force of evil was on the rise day by day, killing and beheading men, women and children in their homes, schools, universities, hospitals, and even on the highways. Every day, ISIS, the Taliban and other terrorist groups would attack anything that represented light, progress or civility, from schools to universities, to libraries, and even places of worship and hospitals. As this violence rose and spread, so did the number of protests against them. I remembered watching another popular protest online some months earlier where tens of thousands marched on the streets of Kabul demanding justice for Shukria Tabassum, who had been kidnapped and beheaded after months of abuse and torture at the hands of ISIS monsters.

Shukria Tabassum had been born in 2006 in a remote village in central Afghanistan to a family who belonged to the Hazara ethnic group. On 9 November 2015 she was brutally beheaded, together with nine other innocent people from her community as they were trying to cross through Kandahar and Shajoy, a district of Zabul Province, a decades-old slaughter point for people like Shukria and her family. It's the same crossing point that I had crossed into the outside world some fifteen years earlier. At the time it was the stronghold of the Taliban before they were removed from power by the US and NATO. However, the terrorists regrouped, and had grown strong enough to kidnap and kill passengers along the way. Following the beheading of Shukria, thousands of young people marched along Kabul streets towards the presidential palace while carrying the beheaded body of the nine-year-old on their shoulders. Outside the palace they demanded peace, justice and security for the vulnerable, including women and girls. For weeks I could not stop imagining how such a horrific event could have happened. The men in their long black robes, their beards and turbans. The noise of them shouting *ALLAHU AKBAR! ALLAHU AKBAR!* as the blades came down, as they became soaked in blood. *ALLUHU AKBAR!* as they reached for the next victim.

I watched a video of young woman called Farkhunda being burned alive on the streets of Kabul as a crowd of men attacked her, reciting these same words: *ALLAHU AKBAR, ALLAHU AKBAR!* The first time I had heard those holy words was as a child, during prayers, and it filled me with pulsating anger to see the words used again and again as weapons of death, fear and destruction.

One morning I woke up to the news that Britain had voted to leave the EU, with immigration and the control of borders a key issue, including the threat of Turkey joining the EU. During my time in the UK, I had seen first-hand the escalation in hostility towards immigrants as front page after front page screamed about the dangers that dehumanised multitudes of people like me, Farzana and Alan. Far-right populist politicians across Europe and America exploited the refugee crisis to further their own agendas.

Throughout my stay in Greece, I heard versions of the same horrific story from people from around the world – almost always of monsters coming to the village with guns. Afghanistan to Syria, Iraq to Somalia, heartless extremist killers like the Taliban, ISIS and Al-Qaida were brutally murdering innocents in cold blood, causing thousands upon thousands to flee for safety. Moving from one place to the next. Separated from family. Preyed on by militants or traffickers or the police. People dying around them. None of the refugees I spoke to had come to Greece with any plan. They were exhausted. Some wanted to try to get further into Europe if they had family there. Or if they knew of somewhere there were communities of their people. But most just wanted to be allowed to stay somewhere they would be safe. They had heard of this new place of hope and sanctuary in the heart of Europe. It was called Germany, a country led by a powerful leader and a legendary heroine, and her name was Angela Merkel. Almost everyone in those overcrowded emergency refugee camps knew her name. She had suddenly become a rare beacon of hope, courage and compassion for some of the world's most vulnerable women, children and men who had fled death and destruction in their own homes and communities across the Middle East, Asia and Africa.

A colleague of mine circulated a poem that I couldn't stop thinking about by the poet Warsan Shire, which had the line: 'No one leaves home, unless home is the mouth of a shark.'

22

Kigali, Rwanda, 2016

'Hello, hello is that you, Arman?' a familiar voice trembled on the other end of the line. This was followed by a pause. A long pause. Then, the sound of some suppressed sobbing. It was my second night at a hotel in the capital Kigali, Rwanda when my phone started ringing just before midnight. I answered it immediately without thinking.

'It's me, Asad,' he whispered. 'Where are you?' he asked.

'Rwanda, Africa,' 'I replied.

'Oh, OK,' followed by another long silence. But I could hear him blowing his nose.

'Hello. Hello. Please tell me what's going on' I insisted.

'I'm sorry. I am so sorry to bring you this sad news,' his voice shivered.

'What is going on? Please tell me,' I begged. The line remained silent. But I could hear him blowing his nose again.

'Sadly, our father passed away this morning,' he announced.

'Stroke,' he added. But my mind had already departed somewhere else. An empty place. An endless vacuum covered in a thick fog of immense sorrow. I cannot remember how long I had been in such a state but Asad cleared his throat. Again. 'May his soul rest in peace,' he said regaining his voice. But I remained there immovable. Silent. Speechless.

'Well, the funeral ceremony is tomorrow. I don't suppose you can make it, can you?' he asked. *Funeral? What funeral? What can't I attend?* These words echoed in waves in this sorrow-filled vacuum. But this feeling was not new. It was familiar. I was somehow expecting something bad happening. Just the night before I had a dream. I was back in the valley and saw a huge object like a passenger plane suddenly appearing from behind the mountain peak just opposite the house before it struck our warn-out home, destroying it.

I suddenly woke up panting and sweating on my hotel bed in Kigali, in the middle of the night. I was pleased that it was not real. That it was just a dream. But deep down I could feel that it was not just a dream. There was something wrong, somewhere, somehow, I was expecting it. Expecting bad news at any moment. The following day no matter what I did or where I went around Kigali, that thick sorrow-filled fog of sadness never left me. It followed me everywhere, like a ghost. So, such a phone call was already expected.

'Impossible,' I responded. 'I don't have my passport with me at the moment. It's with the Rwandan Immigration Department to process my foreign resident permit to be able to work here as an expat,'. I uttered.

'And even if I had my passport, it wouldn't be possible to make travel arrangements in such short notice and travel all the way back in time for the funeral tomorrow,' I added.

'That's what I thought,' he said before saying, 'I got to go. Goodbye.'

I remained there frozen on my hotel bed with the phone held tight against my ear. God knows for how long. I remained in that position without moving with one elbow resting on the pillow and bed frame and the other still holding the phone tight as my thoughts travelled thousands of miles back to the mountains where I was born: mum, Farrukh, Taj, our rooster, chickens, cows, lambs, and never-ending cold winters followed by frightening summers and the sounds of weapons breaking at random times of the night or the day as they wished while mum and I huddled together, praying for them to go away before a bullet hit one of us.

I remembered how, for years I thought my father was that framed picture on the wall. Immortal. Immovable and watching over us until one day he shocked me by appearing as a real person with arms and limbs before disappearing again as another conflict broke out.

So, the first time he talked to me, I mean really talked to me it was in 2008 when I rushed back home after the US and NATO troops had removed the Taliban and installed a new government in place leading to some levels of peace and security in the country. So, as soon as I was able, I went back home. I found Dad at one end of the valley with a few people waiting after they had heard some news arriving from the nearby villages. He was barely recognisable. He seemed in as much shock and disbelief to see me returning alive as I was to see him. He had aged and grown grey hair, a grey beard, and had wrinkles around his eyes and even the back of his hands as he extended them towards me to embrace me and held me in his arms for a few moments. Probably it was the first time ever that I had been that close to Dad.

I didn't see Mum anywhere among the small crowd of people from the village gathering to greet me at the beginning of the valley. I was already getting worried. Before I even said anything, Dad noticed my worry and said, 'Don't worry, your mum is also still alive and well but she couldn't walk all the way to this end of the valley to meet you. As we travelled up the valley, more and more villagers from each side of the river joined. Perhaps they were shocked at what they were seeing. When I arrived closer to our house, I noticed Mum on the side of the river waiting impatiently. As soon as I saw her, I could not hold back any more. I broke down. In her arms. She held me tight. For a moment we both cried together as others waited and watched over us. 'We need to stop, my dear son,' I heard her whispering in my ears. 'It's OK for me to cry but it's not OK for you. You are a youn man now. You've grown well mashallah,' she said, smiling. I stopped.

Many people from up and down the valley accompanied us for the evening. More people from near and far arrived at our house in the following days, to welcome a long-lost member of the community who they thought was no longer alive. After a couple of weeks of welcoming and greeting by numerous family friends and relatives, near and far, one evening, Dad, Mum and a number of elders from the village gathered and opened a conversation. A difficult conversation. I could sense it from the arrivals of some elders from up and down the village. Dad began his speech. One of the things he was known for: speaking well. God brings us to this world as he chooses, and he takes us away as he wishes. And how we should all be grateful for whatever Allah decides for us. Then Dad started mentioning the names of a number of close family members, relatives, who were no longer with us. Some died of natural causes, some were killed inside the country during the war, some lost their lives on the run across border crossings as they tried to cross into neighbouring countries.

The long list of the deceased included my stepbrother, Mohammad, Mum's brother, Dad's brothers, two of them, and the list went on and on including many more brothers, fathers, mothers and sisters, aunts and uncles from the valley that had vanished. Some were still missing while their families still anxiously waited and prayed that their loved ones too would one day turn up alive and well. Me turning up had created some hope. I remained there in shock, unable to fully comprehend the enormity of the loss of lives. 'I understand it must be difficult for you to hear about all these many losses of our loved ones and we all mourn their deaths, but we should all be grateful for those who are still with us. Still alive. Just like yourself. We would have never imagined that in our wildest dreams this day would come to see you alive and well here. But here you are. Miracles do happen. Sometimes. That's what we should be thankful for. The people who are still with us. And may God bless all those who passed away.' He muttered in prayers as other elders took turns to speak along the same lines.

When I tried to dig down for more details about how, when, and why all these people had vanished, Dad quickly intervened and said, 'God chooses however he takes his people away. There is no need to get into the details of their deaths. There are way too many to go through if we go along that path. But we should be grateful that we have you and the rest of us still with us. That's what we should focus on and be grateful for,' he concluded.

Dad explained that normally the tradition is that if any family in the valley loses a loved one, it's expected that others in the valley attend the funeral if they are around. Those who are away must go to their houses for a *fatiha* and pay their respects on their return. But in my case considering the enormity of loss that almost every family up and down the valley including ourselves have suffered it would take us a long time to go around to each individual family to pay our respects. It would be practically impossible, he said. Therefore, the first thing we should do is make an announcement that in the interests of everyone, we would call this tradition off on this particular occasion. This means we neither expected anyone to come for a *fatiha* to us for our losses nor should others expect us to go to them. We want it to be a mutual understanding between us all without anyone getting upset.

However, he added that everyone is welcome to come for a visit and celebration. Not mourning. In the coming days, a couple of times I tried to ask how he himself and the remaining members of the family had survived but he would quickly redirect the conversation to the present or future. 'It was difficult times indeed but thank God that those days have now passed,' he said and 'a new hope for peace and stability has finally been created in this country after all those dark years. That's what we should focus on. The bright side of things and celebrate what we still have with us and hopefully a better future for everyone in this valley and country.'

'Things have changed since the intervention of the international community here. There has been a lot of progress. 'Now we have democracy and a national constitution that gives equal rights to everyone, including minorities and women. Now everyone competes for social and political opportunities like becoming a member of parliament, a minister or even president,' he would say. 'And we all have the right to vote, get an education and participate in social and political processes in the country,' he would say enthusiastically.

When my summer holiday was coming to an end and it was time for me to return to the UK to continue my studies, one evening Dad said, 'We are so grateful to all those kind people in the UK who saved you and gave you a second chance but if you weren't in the middle of your university education, there would be no need for you to go back to the UK any more. We have everything here now. We have peace and security.

So, I would suggest as soon as you finish your studies, you should come back and serve your own people in this country. With that education of yours, you could do anything: become a member of parliament, a minister, or even president – who knows?' he would list optimistically. I flew back to the UK and resumed my studies just in time to start my second year in September.

The next time I saw Dad, it was in 2014. He looked even more tired, resigned even. He was no longer so optimistic about the future of the country. 'The international troops are leaving. And as soon as they leave, the same nightmare will return to this goddamn land,' he would say with certainty. Although there were talks of the US and NATO troops leaving Afghanistan and the people had started worrying about the nightmare of the 1990s returning, no one would say with such certainty that the Taliban could retake the entire country, or the US would leave Afghanistan altogther. Some would speculate that the US and NATO would never leave. That they were just threatening the leader of the Afghan Government to get what they want. That's all. Some would hypothesise that even if the international troops left, the US-trained Afghan army may still be capable enough to stand against the threats caused by the rising insurgencies. However, it was quite clear that a new but very familiar wave of fear had already begun moving rapidly across the country, refreshing the painful and traumatic memories of the 1990s and forcing an increasing number of people to flee the country, contributing to the so called European Refugee Crisis in 2015 and 2016.

I can't remember how long it was that I had remained frozen on the hotel bed in a one-sided position as my mind travelled thousands of miles back home and then back with my phone still held tight in my hand and the memories of Dad circulating in my head from the first day I could remember anything as a child to the present moment. The little memories I had of Dad were mostly of his absence.

I slowly shifted underneath my duvet trying to fall asleep at some point, but I could not. I felt like the world around me was shrinking, tightening to the point I was finding myself out of breath. I jumped out of bed and walked around the room trying to inhale some air. But everything felt suffocating. I rushed out of the hotel in the middle of the night or was it the early hours of the morning? I cannot remember. I had lost all sense of time. For a moment I stood just outside the hotel's main door, looking into the sky and inhaling some fresh air. But the thoughts of going back to the room felt incredibly suffocating.

So, I started walking down the empty and quiet streets of Kigali. It was so quiet that the entire city felt haunted. At the end of that street, I turned into another street and then another until I found myself near a water fountain located on top of a little hill with some streetlights around it. For a moment I stood near the fountain and watched the water falling. The sound of falling water and the early morning breeze made me feel slightly easier on the chest. I could breathe, again. I moved back a few steps and found a wooden bench. I sat on it with my arms crossed around me, still watching the falling water. I must have fallen asleep there at some point to the sound of the water. The cold early morning breeze woke me up. I felt cold, numb. I could see the sky above Kigali lightening. The thoughts of going back to the hotel room didn't feel as suffocating as it had just hours earlier in the night. But now I had no idea where my hotel was or how to get there. So, I walked round and round the empty streets until it was almost bright. The people were out, going about their day-to-day businesses, so I could ask them how to get to my hotel.

That day passed and I was in such a confused state of mind. The following night, as soon as it began to get dark, my suffocating breathlessness would return. The hotel room felt haunted. I could no longer bear the thought of going back to sleep in the same room. Ever again. So, I went to the reception desk and asked to change not just my room but the entire block altogether. They moved me to another block. I felt slightly better there. But still, I had trouble falling asleep at night. So, I got into a routine of either walking around the hotel room or walking out of the hotel altogether and walking the streets all night, getting lost for most of the night. I was gone for hours on end walking the streets on my own, feeling numb and unaware of myself or my surroundings. As these sorrowful moments of solitude continued for a couple of weeks, I could hear myself talking on the streets in the middle of the night. After a couple of weeks, the UN finally completed processing my registration and induction before moving me on to my duty station to begin my new role as child protection officer at one of the world's oldest refugee camps in Africa located on the isolated hills of Rwanda to help refugee children and young people whose lives had been torn apart by war and conflict.

23

Refugee Camp, Rwanda

Baraka must have been nineteen or twenty when I met him in the camp in Rwanda. He was tall, thin young man with high cheekbones and bushy eyebrows. He had been born in a tiny tin-roofed mud hut, one of hundreds of other mud huts that had been sheltering over seventeen thousand displaced men, women and children since 1996. This is where, for the first time, Baraka opened his big brown eyes and stared at the ceiling of his young mother's mud hut, sitting on the uneven red soft mud gradually sliding underneath it. This is where Baraka tasted his first Ugali, a scarce dish made from maize mixed with salt, his only source of food provided by the humanitarian organisations. As he gradually learned how to crawl, his wandering eyes caught sight of the dry riverbed, just outside the hut, which occasionally flooded after torrential rain. During this rainy season, it would get filled with tons of waste water that had passed through hundreds of huts higher up the hill, carrying household waste mixed with red Rwandan soil.

The fast-moving waste water travelled down the dirty river-bed with so much life and energy and Baraka became curious enough to explore what the world had for him outside of his mother's quiet hut. One day he crawled down the slippery mud to touch the fast-moving water to feel its lively currents.

He could see many more mud huts, just the same as his mother's, in the opposite rows and beyond. Once he learned how to crawl out, he kept crawling up and down the riverbed inch by inch, exploring the world around him until his young mother came home and put him back inside the hut.

Over time, as he grew older, he learned that a smile appeared on his mother's tired face only once a month, usually at the beginning of the month. When that day finally arrives, he sees a glimpse of happiness and excitement not only on the faces of his own mum, but on many other mums and children in the neighbouring huts, as if everyone was waiting to smile on that day only. In the morning of that day, like everyone else he wakes up early, gets ready quickly and follows his mum, carrying their empty bags and containers, towards one of the taller hills, near the secondary school, in the middle of the camp. It is called the Food Distribution Centre. There, he sees thousands of other men, women and children from all over the camp waiting in long queues for hours and hours with their containers on their heads and their documents in their hands, waiting for their turn to arrive.

When their turn finally arrives, and they receive their rations of maize, salt and soup to survive on for the rest of the month, he then follows his mother back down the hill, following thousands of other parents and children. In the evening, he watches his mum preparing Ugali with a rare hint of happiness. The aromatic smell of cooking a meal for the night injects a rare atmosphere of warmth and some excitement in their little hut and on his mum's face. He loved seeing her happy, smiling. *Why can't it be like this all the time?* he wondered.

After dinner, his mum tells him some stories from the past and about her childhood. Stories about their village back home in the Congo where once upon a time she lived peacefully with her parents in a beautiful village south of Lake Kivu. She would tell him about the number of cows, goats and donkeys they once owned and how Baraka's grandma milked the goats, fed the hens and collected eggs. And how she would help her mum to bake bread, enough for the entire family all year round. However, one night that all changed when men with guns attacked their village, killing anyone in their way and destroying their homes, forcing Baraka's grandparents to run for their lives across deserts with minefields and wild bushes, before they crossed Lake Kivu into Rwanda. Baraka loved to listen to his mother's stories, even the terrifying ones.

He would often wonder what his life would have been like if war had never found its way to his parents' and grandparents' village. He would picture himself strolling in his grandmother's farm, playing in the green field or helping his grandma to feed their animals during the day, with plenty of delicious food, milk and goat meat, gathering together for meals with Grandpa, his parents, maybe siblings and cousins – one big, happy family. He would wonder why they couldn't go back to their own country. So, one evening he turned to his mother and asked, 'Why can't we go back, Mum?'

'Go where?'

'Back to Congo?'

'Because the war never ended, Baraka. The war never ended.' His mother spat the words out of her mouth with such bitterness. 'We never imagined ourselves still being here in this refugee camp after all these years . . . all these years,' she repeated. 'But there you go,' she muttered as she shrugged her slumping shoulders. *The war never ended, Baraka. The war never ended.*

The war never ended, Baraka repeated under his tongue, but asked no more questions that evening. However, those words stuck with him for the following days, weeks, months and even years, thinking about peace. As he got older, like thousands of other uprooted children and young people he would wander around the camp and see more and more children like himself from the same country and in the same situation with the same problems. *The war never ended, Baraka. the war never ended.* Sometimes, when they went up to the Food Distribution Centre, he would see a few people with different-coloured skin, in different clothes and footwear, some holding a shiny camera in their hands, taking multiple photos of anything: the mud huts, the wandering children and the old and wrinkled men sitting on the soft soil and dust in front of their huts, waiting.

Whenever Baraka suspected a camera was pointed in his direction, he would try to display his best poses, just in case a shot of him was captured among the crowd. He would never see the photos of him taken on their expensive cameras or smartphones. Often, he would join other children to follow those visitors, chasing them up and down the camp until they jumped back into their white Land Cruisers and drove away. Sometimes, Baraka and his friends would chase the cars until they were stopped by the camp guards at the barrier entry and exit point that they could not cross. They would watch the vehicles driving up the hill until they became as small as a beetle, disappearing into a world beyond. A world he had never been to and only knew through his mother's stories.

In the evening, when the hot sun would sink behind the faraway hills on the other side of Lake Kivu, he would return to his mum's mud hut, itching to tell her about what he had seen up in the camp: the white Land Cruiser, the *muzungu* (white) people with shiny and expensive cameras in their hands, taking lots of photos, but still she rarely shared his excitement.

Gradually, as time passed, Baraka and his friends started to grow tired of their only adventure – chasing foreign humanitarian workers or visitors in their white cars. Over the years, the unfamiliar facial expressions, the ingenuine smiles and the countless clicks of cameras through the window of their luxurious Land Cruisers had changed nothing for them in the camp. They remained in the same mud huts, with the same fences, the same hunger. The gloomy look on his mother's face, the deep ravine-like wrinkles on the exhausted, worn-out faces of the elders and the grim, depressive air of hopelessness among his friends spoke to the helplessness of their situation and the passing of years where nothing had improved. The desolation engulfed the entire camp, taking Baraka down into its darkness.

In the mornings, as the sun rose from behind a tall hill only a few hundred metres away, east of the camp, he would witness hundreds of grandmas and grandpas quietly tottering out of their overcrowded and dust-ridden mud huts, with the help of their worn-down walking sticks, and them sitting outside on the dust. All day they would have nothing to do but watch their children and grandchildren, the latter still filled with youthful energy, playing in the dust on the dirt roads, unaware of their fate, their destiny, to live in a suffocating refugee camp crammed with tens of thousands of men, women and children trapped indefinitely on the remote hills of Western Rwanda, far away from civilisation with no hope or future.

One day, one of Baraka's friends introduced him to a group of young people who invited him to join their kung-fu club. It was being organised by a young man called Baptist who had set it up not just to practise kung fu himself but also teach other young people in the camp to help strengthen their minds and bodies against increasing despair, hunger and hopelessness. Baraka knew little about those kinds of sports, but he joined anyway since he had nothing else to do. After the first couple of sessions, he felt something different, something easing the heavy weight, the tension in his aching shoulders, back and neck. Even the occasional dark cloud of fog in his tired mind somehow seemed to soften up. Just to relieve the pain and tension, he continued going to practise kung fu with his new friends, but then his instructor told him that to continue practising in the club, he would have to pay 100 Rwandan francs (about six pence in British sterling). When he revealed the news to his mum, she told him they could not pay that amount and Baraka was left with no choice but to drop his kung-fu club.

Now, having nothing else to do, Baraka fell back into his old routine, wandering around the camp aimlessly and watching the grandmas and grandpas sitting outside their little dusty mud huts, listening to the news on their dust-ridden old radios, waiting indefinitely for peace to come to their home country or for their resettlement to a new country to arrive. He worried he would become them. As these thoughts hung heavily on him with feelings of there being nowhere else to turn, Baraka became caught in the killer claws of despair, which had already grabbed many of his friends by the throat, leading them to spiral into substance abuse, depression and hopelessness.

One day, as he wandered around the camp, he met one of his former kung-fu club friends, who told him that someone from the UNHCR office called Arman had visited their kung-fu club and had promised to support the club so that everyone who wanted to join the club could practise for free. First, Baraka laughed. Like his parents, grandparents and everyone else in the camp, he had heard it all before. They had said that the food rations would increase; that resettlement services to a third country would be expedited; that more educational opportunities and youth empowerment would be provided for more young people and so on. Despite these promises, nothing much had improved in the camp.

Even though Baraka had his doubts, he joined the club since there was nothing else for him to do anyway. He discovered that not only did he not have to pay tuition fees, but also every member of the club was to be given sports equipment and a professional instructor was coming from outside of the camp to assist. When he witnessed the fresh changes, he became more interested, and he attended his classes regularly. However, when he told his mum and elders in the camp, they laughed at him.

Despite joining the club, Baraka's mental health continued to hang in the balance. Although a glimpse of fresh hope was refreshing, it wasn't quite enough to lift the powerful atmosphere of despair, hopelessness and cynicism which had been engulfing the entire camp for decades. Baraka continued to float in between the three emotions until the end of the year when something unbelievable happened. He watched a handful of his teammates leave the camp to take part in a national competition and then return with championship medals: a gold, a silver and a bronze medal, proudly hanging from around their necks, in a camp of thousands of children and young people who had never been beyond the camp barrier. They all returned with countless stories about their journey into the outside world – stories about life outside the camp, about cars moving on the paved streets and streetlights lighting everywhere. Stories about the national competition taking place in the famous Mahoro Centre in the heart of the rising capital city Kigali, where high-profile national and international tournaments would take place every year – a place that Baraka and other young people in the camp wouldn't even dream of being able to visit, let alone have the chance to compete in person against national teams and win national championship medals. Stories that no other young person in the camp had ever experienced or even dreamt of up to that point. Baraka, his friends, and thousands of other young people suddenly woke up to an unlikely glimpse of hope. They wish they had joined the kung-fu club earlier and had practised harder so that they too could have been among the young contestants. They envied them and regretted how they had missed such a golden opportunity.

At the beginning of the following year, the same opportunities expanded to all young people and covered a wide range of activities: from kung fu, karate, tae kwon do, football, volleyball and basketball to dance, music and theatre. In the first few months, hundreds of young leaders were trained by some of the best professionals in the country while thousands of young people joined various activities with joy, hope and excitement. By the end of the second year, many young contestants, including Baraka, successfully got through provincial tournaments to compete in the national championship in Kigali.

This time around, the contestants returned to the camp with even greater victories, having won over ten championship medals and the national kung-fu championship trophy. The news of the championship trophy being won by an unknown refugee team hidden on the remote hills of western Rwanda dominated all the Rwandan TV channels and newspapers. Overnight, the championship medallists appeared on TV speaking about their success and dreams of becoming international champions with a message of hope and peace throughout the world. On their return to the camp, they were welcomed with open arms by hundreds of friends and family members celebrating their achievements and overnight fame. All of a sudden, the decades-old, depressed refugee camp abandoned and neglected on the isolated hills of western Rwanda turned into an unlikely place of celebration and inspired hope in tens of thousands, and even hundreds of thousands, of displaced refugee youths trapped in camps across the region.

At the same time, the old-age and inevitable news of ration cuts and declining support were looming in the ears of their parents and grandparents who were barely surviving on an extraordinarily limited amount of food each month. Baraka's mother had been hearing all sorts of rumours, including one that the people who had been providing food were planning to starve refugees in the camps. The rumours grew and led to even more chaos and panic among the already malnourished camp population. They gathered together to protest inside the camp to make their voices heard. When they felt their voices were not being heard inside the camp, thousands of men, women and children left the camp without the permission of the authorities and walked down the hill for hours. They camped around the office of the mayor and the UNHCR for three days and nights. The same office I was working in at the time. For our personal security, all staff members were instructed to work from home instead.

And then the shooting began.

24

Refugee Camp, Rwanda

The sound of machine-gun fire exploded through the air. I rushed outside my guarded accommodation and ran towards the edge of the high concrete wall, topped by coils of barbed wire. The gunfire went on for several minutes, silencing the children I had heard singing and laughing. Goats and cows milled around in the bushes and their silhouettes broke the colourful streaks of mist, dust and haze as the sun set over the high hills on the other side of Lake Kivu, barely visible to the naked eye. I could just about see it from the top of a hill that I had been calling home for the last eighteen months, since leaving Greece.

Amid the deafening silence, my distressed gaze caught up with my day guard Peter's puzzled stare, as his dark brown eyes dutifully skimmed over the house for signs of danger. 'The police would have stopped them at the bottom of the hill if they tried to come this way,' he cautiously murmured under his drying lips, still smiling, however anxiously. 'Thanks Peter,' I nodded with a forced smile, unsure of what else to say at that moment. On the inside, mixed emotions coiled in my stomach, just like the coiled barbed wires around the house, carefully installed for my protection. It was not my security that I was worried about but the safety and security of those vulnerable children, women, and men who were under fire from the Rwandan security forces and there was nothing that I could do to save them but listen helplessly to the sounds of machine guns. We both listened anxiously to the one-sided gun battle in the nearby hills for several minutes, followed again by a brief period of silence.

Soon after the deafening silence, a penetrating burst of sorrowful wailing, of babies, children, men and women broke out. It echoed across the hills and moved in multiple waves, getting closer, gradually passing us by to somewhere in the distance – somewhere where there was a camp neglected for decades, far, far away from the eyes of the world.

Long after the painful sounds of sorrowful wailing had disappeared behind the hills and thick shadows of darkness fell over our accommodation, I thought I could still hear the despair. It remained there, still echoing and ringing inside my ears. Their pain was heartbreaking and sorrowful. No matter how hard I would try to sleep, sleep didn't come. I felt sick.

The first time I had heard about the Rwandan genocide, I was still at university in the UK. It was in one of my seminars about peace and conflict resolution. As part of that programme, the Rwandan genocide came up briefly as a case study about the successes and failures of international interventions in keeping the peace. In the case of Rwanda, it was a failure to intervene in time to keep the peace and prevent the atrocities that followed. I learned that prior to the genocide, the international community, under the leadership of the United Nations, had dispatched a small number of peacekeepers to monitor the peace between the two warring ethnic groups: The Hutu, who dominated the Rwandan government, and the Tutsi rebels.

However, when systematic violence began unfolding up and down the country, the United Nations Peacekeepers found themselves cornered in the rapidly escalating conflict without having the required support or authority to intervene to stop the massacres. Instead, they stood by and watched the genocide happen before their very eyes as hundreds of thousands of innocent children, men and women were butchered to death with machetes and bullets across Rwanda.

The genocidal campaign by the Hutu extremists to 'exterminate' the Tutsis from Rwanda lasted for about a hundred days and allegedly about 800,000–1,000,000 predominantly Tutsi men, women and children were massacred over those hundred days. The genocide only ended when the Tutsi rebels closed in from the north of the country, eventually liberating the country from the hands of the genocidaires. The new Tutsi-dominated government, together with renewed support from the international community, set up local, national and international tribunal courts to bring the perpetrators to justice and established some level of peace and justice in the country. For a better understanding of the context, I had read some textbooks and watched some brief video clips about the Rwandan genocide. And now those video clips which I had seen over a decade ago were replaying live in my head:

The fresh blood dripping from the tip of thousands of long machetes frantically attacking homes, villages, towns and cities in a brutal killing frenzy up and down the many thousands of hills across Rwanda; sliced-up arms, legs and other body parts dumped and drowned in a sea of blood across the neighbourhoods: homes, huts, churches and mosques turning from a place of worship, community and unity into violent human slaughterhouses containing thousands of human body parts. Friends turning on friends. Partners turning against partners. Even religious leaders like priests secretly leading their prayers to encourage deaths in their own churches. No one would be spared, not even children, as long as they were Tutsi.

ACROSS MOUNTAINS, LAND AND SEA

The western parts of Rwanda, where I had now been based for the last eighteen months, had been one of the worst-hit areas where thousands and thousands of men, women and children were brutally killed. Now, shivering underneath my duvet, I hated to think of how many innocent men and women might've been killed on the hill that I was now calling home. The whole thing felt as fresh as the evening before, listening to the wailing and mourning of thousands of Congolese refugee women, men and children, shot dead by the Tutsi-dominated Rwandan security forces. How could this country, so recently desecrated by violence, bring violence upon another vulnerable community?

When I arrived in Kigali in August 2016, I was still waiting for the UNHCR country office to facilitate my travel to take up my post at my new duty station, west of the country, so I had some time on my hands to explore the city. One day I joined a group of other international visitors to visit a few genocide centres, including the Kigali Memorial Centre, where the remains of over 250,000 murdered men, women and children are still neatly piled up on display for visitors. A polite Rwandan lady welcomed us into the centre and guided us down some narrow, steep steps into the underground, leading us through aisles of thousands and thousands of butchered human skulls neatly piled up on each side.

'That's where the machetes hit.' she said, pointing at the broken part of the skulls. 'This part was cut through by machetes.' 'And that's the bullet wounds,' pointing at the missing part of the skulls here and there along the aisles, as she led us through. Following the rest of the group, I continued walking along the aisles of the butchered human skulls quietly, like the other visitors. However, on the inside, I struggled to contain the powerful waves of feelings, thoughts and countless questions about the horrors of wars and conflict, and the capability of human beings to heartlessly massacre almost a million other human beings in just one hundred days.

It was my first time visiting a genocide centre and seeing the evidence of such atrocities, and I thought of the affinity the Tutsi had with my own people, the Hazaras, who were similarly almost wiped out

In Rwanda, the genocide commemoration begins every April and continues for a hundred days to mark the 1994 genocide against the Tutsis. During this period, the entire country mourns the tragic loss of lives during the genocide in unity and raises the famous slogan: NEVER AGAIN. While the Tutsi genocide in Rwanda quickly became recognised as one of the world's most brutal in recent human history, on a par with the Holocaust, the Hazara Genocide and systematic oppression that has continued for well over a hundred years has remained one of the world's most silenced atrocities in human history. A secret kept well. *How could it ever be possible,* I've always wondered?

I must have fallen asleep at some point while my head was still filled with all these graphic thoughts and memories. And when I woke up in the morning, I found a text message from my boss telling me that the office was now open and that everyone should return to the office.

In the following days and weeks, together with my colleagues, I worked long hours to help deal with the aftermath of the incident and the casualties left behind by the shooting.

Baraka's name was among the list of over a dozen men, women and children shot and killed by Rwandan security forces during the massacre. I had been working at the camp for eighteen months, and seeing these familiar names on the list broke me. I remember the last time I saw Baraka. He had presented part of an end-of-year project evaluation workshop in the camp, just a couple of months before.

'I want to use the power of my sports to bring peace in Congo and around the world,' Baraka had said. Another young championship medallist said: 'We want to become a peace leader because no one can appreciate peace more than us – refugees.' 'I want to become an international kung-fu champion so that I can use my voice for peace and justice,' another national championship gold medallist added. 'I want to become a film director so that I can use my skills to promote peace around the globe,' said a young woman. The scenes replayed in my head, every word; their hopes and dreams for a peaceful and just world. But for Baraka and dozens of his fellow young refugees killed or injured by the Rwandan security forces, that world would never materialise. Their lives were short and brutish. Baraka was buried nameless because no one – not even his mother – could identify his shattered face, torn apart by bullets.

When I thought of my years working with refugees, it was the sound of crying children I thought of. Crying from hunger and fear. Crying because they missed their families. Those people I met, their lives in pieces, displaced, suffering and lost, would flood out of the wall with the people I had lost on my own journey. My wall had collapsed, and I was faced with the crying voices of little children like nine-year-old Shukria Tabassum, captured, tortured and beheaded by terrorists after months of torture in captivity in the highway of southern Afghanistan; the pleading cries of Farkhunda being burned alive in broad daylight on the streets of Kabul; the hundreds of little boys blown up by bombs in their classrooms, with their books pressed hard against their little bleeding chests in western Kabul; of Baraka; and of the boys I had known and left behind; of the ones who never made it.

I would hear Nemat's pleading voice on the dinghy: 'I don't want to die. I want to see my mother again. Please, God, help me this time and this time only . . .' while floating on the violent wings of storm waves in the Mediterranean Sea. I would see Anwar's dark brown eyelids struggling to remain open as if the unbearable weight of the universe was pushing them down, as he stayed trapped in so-called community detention in Australia, living in limbo.

I could hear the voices of young Yazidi girls caught, raped and sold as sex slaves across Iraq; the voices of Rohingya children maimed and killed in their homes and villages in Myanmar. The little lifeless body of Alan Kurdi, a two-year-old Syrian boy washed ashore on a Turkish beach, lying upside down and drowned together with his elder brother Ghalib and his mother, in the hope of finding peace in some corner of the world, but like tens of thousands of other displaced children, women and men, they lost their lives in stormy seas. One tragic story of a lost soul would take my mind directly to the next tragic story. Non-stop.

Those thoughts of lost lives, silenced voices and shattered dreams of those who had simply wanted a peaceful and hopeful future, were impacting my sleep, appetite for food and joy of life. So, during the weekends, while other expats and Rwandan colleagues would drive up to Kigali or disperse around the country and region to meet friends and family, I would spend my time alone, either jogging on the hills or sitting and staring at the famous Lake Kivu for hours. This lake is famous for all sorts of reasons. I'd heard some frightening stories about it: that the lake was approximately 400–450 metres deep and that, unlike its calm appearance on the surface, there were powerful undercurrents and movements underneath it that could mysteriously claim the lives of people swimming in it. I would often hear news of people drowning in the lake, overcome by its currents. Just like Lake Kivu, there were forces and currents moving within me that felt beyond my control, and the longer I kept things suppressed, the more dangerous the situation was becoming for me.

I could feel my chest tightening, my breath shortening and my voice disappearing inside my drying throat as if the pressure of those experiences, memories and information were all happening there and then – all at the same time. As these emotions kept growing deeper and stronger, I would often find myself tired, frustrated and questioning everything, and criticising national and international policies for leading to such endless injustices and suffering, while wondering what else I could do to help relieve suffering and injustices.

However, somewhere in the corner of my brain, I could hear other voices, some of which were friends and colleagues, reassuring me and embracing me. Telling me that the world cannot be changed by just one person; that I was already doing a lot by providing lifesaving programmes for vulnerable people; that I should focus on myself, my health and potentially great prospects ahead of me, and not overwhelm myself with the things I cannot change.

The vast majority of us get upset when we see grave injustices and suffering around us but hesitate to speak up or do anything about it because we're worried about the consequences it might have for us – for our jobs, our security, our future. Or we just feel powerless and overwhelmed. So, we simply try to carry on, turning a blind eye to the injustices and suffering around us. While all these are understandable, at the same time, wouldn't such inaction inadvertently help the monsters to continue causing chaos, suffering, and injustices around the world with impunity? Wouldn't we be living in a better world if we all stood up or at least did something? Perhaps things as simple as raising awareness or telling a story? Spreading the word or telling the story of those who cannot tell it themselves can be one of the most powerful things ever because the first thing that oppressed people lose is their voice. And that's when despicable atrocities will happen to them – silently and with impunity. I remembered a quote by Martin Luther King Jr that said: 'The ultimate tragedy is not the oppression and cruelty by the bad people, but the silence over that by the good people.' With this in mind and as much as how difficult it was to revisit the traumatic stories I had come across both in my personal and professional life so far, one evening I took a pen and a piece of paper and started writing.

25

Geneva, Palace des Nations

'Ladies and gentlemen, today I am here to speak to you, not just as your colleague but also as a former refugee and an asylum seeker.' As I uttered these words, my eyes quickly surveyed the reactions of the silent audience staring at me from behind their desks. I licked my dry lips and my stomach flipped over.

In December 2016, the United Nations High Commissioner for Refugees entitled its annual conference 'Children on the Move'. The entire two-day conference was to discuss the plight of children fleeing war zones alone, embarking on deadly and dangerous journeys from Africa and the Middle East towards Europe and North America in search of safety. Millions of refugees, including tens of thousands of unaccompanied children, had been forced to flee their homes, communities and worn-torn countries, most of them from Syria, Afghanistan, Iraq, Sudan and Somalia; crossing through the intense heat of the Sahara Desert in Africa and the stormy Mediterranean Sea around Europe.

As a former unaccompanied child myself, and now as an international humanitarian practitioner, striving to protect vulnerable children in desperate situations, often in dangerous and remote parts of the world, I was invited to give insight into the situation of these unaccompanied children on the move across borders to an audience that consisted of government representatives, UN leaders and heads of NGOs. I thought it was a good opportunity for me to speak on behalf of millions of displaced children across the world who have lost their homes, families and countries, many of whom died, drowned or continue suffering in silence in dire conditions around the world.

In the room were a group of people who had the power to set policy relating to refugees and asylum seekers. I had spent much time writing a speech that I hoped might communicate just a fraction of what it was like to be an asylum seeker. My audience dealt in statistics and percentages, in tens, hundreds of thousands, millions. And here I was, one person, with many stories of children impacted by war and conflicts. I looked down at the words on the page.

I told them about the children I had met, from when I was a child myself, fleeing Afghanistan, to when I worked for the UN and met so many others with stories like mine. I looked at the audience in front of me, opened my mouth and continued.

'Most of these children will never tell their stories. There are bodies floating in the sea, washed up on beaches, kidnapped, trafficked, murdered by design or by accident. They will never tell their stories.

'Today we are living at a time when an unprecedented number of people are being uprooted from their homes, communities and countries because of senseless wars, causing colossal destruction, devastation and the death of millions of innocent girls, boys, men and women across the world. This happens against the backdrop of the current political climate where politicians and governments are increasingly competing to boost their popularity by cutting aids that are so vital in saving the lives of millions of vulnerable people in desperate situations, while at the same time making billions from the sales of deadly weapons and military capabilities to rogue states and dictators around the world, which are often used to destroy the homes and communities of the very people we call refugees today.

'At this pivotal moment in history, I believe every human being bears a moral responsibility to extend a helping hand into this dark and depressive world of death, destruction and displacement where millions of oppressed and uprooted little girls and boys are suffering in silence. In silence – we don't hear about them because the media has no interest in reporting about them. But we know where they are. They are detained in detention camps or trapped in refugee camps or, even worse, they are abandoned on the streets, jungles, woods, parks and demolished/abandoned buildings exposed to violence, abuse and exploitation.

'In this critical time when the countries are increasingly cutting aid and are turning their backs on tens of millions of uprooted people, it is now the responsibility of every compassionate human being like you to save these innocent lives.

'I believe no child should ever have to suffer because of war, conflict and persecution.

'I believe no child should ever have to die while trying to reach safety, like Alan Kurdi.

'I believe every child, regardless of where they are born or what race, religion or colour of skin they may have, must be protected from abuse, negligence and exploitation, and they must have an opportunity to learn, develop and realise their full potential as free and dignified human beings as created by God.

'If we all do what we must, together we can make a real difference to the lives of millions of uprooted and suffering people. We can heal the wounds of wars. We can give homes to the homeless and hope for the hopeless. Together we can ease suffering and make a real difference in making this world a better and brighter place for everyone, every child and every man and woman to live in peace and with dignity.

'So, let's not give up on the millions of innocent oppressed and and uprooted children and people who die in despair.

'Above all, let's not forget that peace, human rights and humanity are still worth fighting for.'

Arman is currently living in the UK, but he has returned to Afghanistan on a number of occasions and has been reunited with his family.

Acknowledgments

This book would not exist without the unwavering support, sage advice and encouragement of my exceptional agent, Jim Gill, and his brilliant assistant Amber Garvey. A lasting debt of gratitude is owed to you both for your relentless commitment to bringing this project to fruition. Jim Gill, you are the best agent I could have asked for. Thank you for believing in me.

A profound thanks to my wonderful editors, Katie Packer and Jamie Coleman. Your keen insights, meticulous editing, guidance and wisdom have not only refined but elevated this work to new heights. I am particularly appreciative of your kind cooperation and understanding in navigating the necessary adjustments brought about by the sudden changes in circumstances and the considerable complications posed by working with an anonymous author. I truly feel privileged to have worked with you both in this process.

To the whole team at Orion, especially Tierney Witty, Serena Arthur, Yadira Da Trinidade and Francesca Pearce, thank you for your invaluable contribution. Without your hard work and immense talents, this book would not exist.

To my friends, colleagues and all those whom I crossed paths with along this journey, particularly those whose pieces of stories have found their place within these pages, your contributions have enriched this shared narrative and I am thankful for your part in this collective endeavour.

Finally, my eternal thanks and gratitude to all my friends and family for their boundless love, support and faith.